Wisdom's Cry
Through Portals from Heaven

TOMMY (TOMMIE) JACKSON

New International Version (NIV)

Holy Bible, New International Version®, NIV® Copyright ©1973, 1978, 1984, 2011 by Biblica, Inc.® Used by permission. All rights reserved worldwide.

Assisted by: Global Destiny Enterprises, LLC

Cover design by: Angela Mills Camper of Dezign Pro Printing & Graphics

Printed in the United States of America

First Printing, 2021

ISBN: 978-0-578-82906-7

Dedication

This book is dedicated to my daughter, Tiffany Nataya Lindley and my grandson, Jonathan Benjamin Lindley, my children. They are gifts from my God and are true examples of God opening the windows of heaven and pouring out blessings on my life.

My children are a very special part of me. They are more than my children, they are the answer to prayers, inspirations, lessons learned, and true treasures given to me from heaven. I will always love you with a love ordained by God. I love you with the love of a mother.

In loving memory of Tiffany Nataya Lindley. (1980-2001)

Acknowledgements

God in His wisdom lets us know we need each other. With Him placing us at the right places at the right time, a beautiful plan is formed (like a puzzle). He brings all the pieces together.

Myself alone as one piece of that plan would not be complete. But when all the pieces come together and are positioned in their place makes the plan complete. And when that plan is revealed, every piece of it is just as important as the other.

In saying that, I give thanks to My Lord and Saviour Jesus Christ. Without Him none of this would be possible. He walks with and talks with me daily! And teaches me how to hear His voice. Which makes this journey called life something it could never be without Him! When He speaks, my hand becomes the pen of a ready writer! O how He loves us!

And to the rest. Because of your obedience to the one who orchestrated the plan (God the Father); the plan is complete.

So, our deepest thanks are extended to you:

Jesse V. Jackson, my husband, friend and love. You were sent to me when I needed you most. You were a tool to show me there was life after loss, and an aid in my healing. We realized we were answers to each other's prayers. Thank you for being who you were supposed to be in this plan, a very special and one of the most important parts, whom I love and appreciate dearly.

My Mother for always praying with and for us.

Pastor Delmus and Stephanie Gillis (my Pastors). Who constantly reminded me of what God had placed in me, when I could not see it myself.

Jasma Starks, Bonnie Scott, Maurice Morris, Tajuana Perry and Isaiah Vaughn for always being willing and ready to help in any way they can.

Edith White and Dennis Johnson, your words of encouragement were the push that kept me going when I almost gave up pursuing God's plan.

And to all those that make up the volume of this book, whom God used without their even knowing, I thank you!

I am truly blessed for all being placed in my life. And I in no way take it for granted. So again, thank you to the pieces of the puzzle that made it complete.

Tommy (Tommie)Jean Jackson

Testimonials

Tommie Jackson has merged her love of God and concern for others into a piece of artistry that speaks to the human condition. In this work, she points the reader to Jesus Christ as the answer to life's problems and the restorer of the human soul. This is a celebration of a child of God who has witnessed and survived the best and the worst of life and still has the joy of her salvation. What a joy it is to be personally connected to this gift to the body of Christ and to witness of the outpouring and overflow of the Holy Spirit in her life. I stand with all those who will read this heartfelt labor of love in saying thank you for letting us share in the intimacy of your relationship with God.

Pastor Delmus L. Gillis II

I had the honor and privilege of previewing this wonderful book! Tommie Jackson has a God given gift of parables. She has the ability to take common everyday situations and her personal experiences to teach practical life lessons. The lessons always direct the reader to Jesus the source of our salvation! I pray God will receive the glory for the work of His obedient servant. This book has blessed me, and I am confident it will bless all who read it!

Stephanie E. Gillis

An inspiring collection of short stories filled with wisdom, knowledge and spiritual growth. Good read. Be blessed!

Edith White

This book, written by my very blessed sister, is an inspiring piece of reading. It lets me know how in all of life's situations God is speaking to us. The question is, are we listening? I know of certain events in this book personally; but I didn't know the power involved in them. As I learn more and more about our Lord and Saviour Jesus Christ, I too am beginning to hear and understand the whisper of Wisdom and knowledge. Thank you, Sis! I love you and God bless!

Dennis Johnson

Table of Contents

Introduction

Fresh and new is how I felt when I was first born again. I was full of enthusiasm. I had a lifetime of questions to ask my Heavenly Father. Learning of Him took priority in my life. The way He operated and how He changed me was such a mystery to me. I had to know. My heart would yearn for wisdom from Him. I was like a sponge longing to be immersed into that fountain of living water. But being a babe in Christ, I was afraid to take that plunge.

You see, as a child, I was always taught that we were not to question God. "Some things are not for us to know" is what the elders would say. So why was there this tugging going on inside of me? Why was I like a student going to school for the first time? I was full of eagerness to learn. It was as if there was this great teacher somewhere beaconing me to come to class and sit under his tutelage to learn. And as strong as the yearning was for me to learn, I felt He had the same yearning to teach.

So, I began to ask of God, looking and listening for answers. It's not that He doesn't want us to ask or that He doesn't answer. He answers us in all sorts of ways. The thing is, do we listen? Do we limit Him in his answering? We must ask ourselves, why do we ask? Do we ask while going through trials as if He doesn't know what He is doing? For some crazy reason, we may ask Him in a scornful manner, "Why me?" As if we deserve something better or an explanation for why we are going through a certain situation. Often, we may ask, not believing He will even answer. But in all our asking, we should ask of Him as student to teacher, knowing He holds the answers.

He can answer any question. He's omniscient, he knows everything. He can answer, however, and with whatever He pleases. In the beginning, He created everything. And everything belongs to Him. He is omnipresent everywhere. He can answer anywhere he pleases. He is omnipotent, all-powerful. He is Omni, all. He is all that He needs to be and all that we need Him to be.

I said all this to say, we can attend different schools to learn various trades, subjects, or achieve different careers that we chose in life. But what school can we attend to learn about life itself? We can learn different theologies and recite various quotes. We can learn about noble men, and some may even get to sit in their presence. There are many teachers and professors in this world recognized for their ability to teach. There are many schools labeled as the school, college or university of the highest degree of learning. But I said to myself, "What an honor it would be to attend the school and sit under the tutelage of the one who created the universe." It would be an honor to be taught by the one who knows all things and mastered all things. The one who holds all wisdom and knowledge in His hands. He is the one who chooses the foolish things of this world to confound the wise. Yes, it would be an honor indeed, because there is no greater teacher.

God in His awesomeness can impart in us and teach us that which man cannot teach. He can reach those whom man cannot reach. Knowing this, one must ask themselves, why is there so much division among God's people? Why so many different beliefs? Often, one may answer, there are different teachers. Others may say because of different upbringings, cultures, etc. Many times, people will answer, "mamma used to say" or "daddy used to say." I myself would often hear my teacher (God in His infinite wisdom) say, "In life's situations, sometimes we need to know more than what man can teach us. With that being said, what if we had such a strong desire to learn all that we could possibly learn to cause us to be a true success in this life? Don't get me wrong, education is good. But what if we could get an education that extends beyond this life, one that will benefit us when we leave this world? The only education that will follow us into eternity. The only one that will really matter, and that will make us a true success.

If we could choose any teacher or any school in the universe with tuition paid in full, what school would we choose? Would it be a small community college with a limited higher learning? Would it be a manmade university (a number of colleges under one administration) also with a limited degree of learning? Or would it be any other institution for learning that you may choose. Although the schools mentioned above do offer a higher education to a certain degree, they all fall short of educating at the highest degree. Or would you choose the school with the teacher (God) of highest degree? A school and teacher that have no limitations of what can be taught.

No man has taught Him; therefore, no man can limit Him in what or how He can teach. He is wisdom and knowledge. I tell you, without a shadow of a doubt, the one mentioned and is usually chosen last is ranked the first. No book could hold all that He teaches me. But just as He opened portals from heaven with Wisdom's Cry for me, I feel it's only proper to share with you.

A Message from the Teacher

Hear, ye children, the instruction of a father, and attend to know understanding. For I give you good doctrine, forsake ye not my law. For I was my father's son, tender and only beloved in the sight of my mother. He taught me also, and said unto me, let thine heart retain my words: keep my commandments and live. Get wisdom, get understanding forget it not; neither decline from the words of my mouth. Forsake her not, and she shall preserve thee: Love her, and she shall keep thee. Wisdom is the principal thing: therefore, get wisdom: and with all thy getting get understanding. Exalt her, and she shall promote thee: she shall bring thee to honor when thou dost embrace her. She shall give to thine head an ornament of grace: a crown of glory shall she deliver to thee.

Proverbs 4:1-9

The Danger Zone

"He said to them, 'Go into all the world and preach the gospel to all creation." *(Mark: 16:15 NIV)*

I t was summer! The time of year everyone seems to enjoy. A time for fun and playing outside for the kids. It's a time when different outside events are scheduled, where there is food, fun, family and friends. This day we had attended one of those events. We played games, ate and participated in other activities at the event. And all the kids got helium-filled balloons.

After all the fun and activities and with our stomachs full, we decided to go to a friend's house for further visiting. My daughter and the other children were outside playing while my friends and I were inside visiting. The youngest of the children was about three years old. She was playing with her balloon. The balloon was swept away from her by the wind and headed towards a busy street. Frantically, the child began crying and chasing the balloon. My daughter Tiffany, seeing the danger of it all, began running after the child, desperately calling out to her. NO! STOP! WAIT! Repeatedly calling out the child's name. Hearing the urgency in my daughter's voice, my friends and I rushed outside to see what was going on.

The mother of the child and my friend started yelling to my daughter, being that they made it outside first, catch her Tiffany, catch her! My daughter yelling back, "I can't," still chasing the young child. As I stepped out the door and realized what was going on, I yelled with all my might, "You Better Catch Her!" The sound of my voice and my daughter realizing who was giving the command seem to invigorate her. She began to pick up strength and speed, running with all her might. It was as if she became Supergirl catching the young child before she reached the danger zone.

Thinking back on that situation a few days later, I thought about how horrible it would have been if my daughter would not have caught the child before reaching the busy street. What if she would not have obeyed my command? What a tragedy it would have been! My heart sank with grief as I envisioned the tragedy happening in my head. At that moment, I realized how important it was for my daughter to hear and obey my voice. Reality set in. How much more important the command the Lord has given us? How much more urgent it is for us to hear and obey His voice? He gave us a command. And he said unto them, "Go ye into all the world and preach the gospel to every creature." (Mark: 16:15). We are to go desperately after those chasing something that will only bring them temporary pleasure; unconsciously headed for the danger zone—chasing something that could cause them to lose their very life, even life eternal.

A Word of Wisdom

How dangerously the spiritually unconscious run.

how desperate the cry of the Heavenly Father,

Who gave His only begotten Son

Who gives us wisdom to understand,

how serious we must take His command.

For with His blood our sins He did atone.

Therefore, we must reach the lost,

before they reach the danger zone.

Watches Over Me

"Keep your lives free from the love of money and be content with what you have, because God has said, 'Never will I leave you: never will I forsake you.'" (Hebrews 13:5 NIV)

"And when he had taken it, the four living creatures and the twenty-four elders fell down before the Lamb. Each one had a harp and they were holding golden bowls full of incense, which are prayers of God's people." (Revelations 5:8 NIV)

"For the eyes of the Lord are on the righteous, and his ears are attentive to their prayer, but the face of the Lord is against those who do evil." (1Peter 3:12 NIV)

Sunday morning, I'd had my time with the Lord. It was time for my daughter and me to get ready for Sunday school and morning worship.

As I held my skirt up to inspect it, I noticed that it was wrinkled. So I set up the ironing board in the kitchen and began to iron it. Like the iron on the skirt, life was pressing hard on me at the time. I was going through a much-unwanted divorce. I was feeling deserted, left alone to raise and care for a child on my own.

I purchased our clothes at an outlet store. They were cheap. The skirt put out an unpleasant odor as the hot iron pressed hard on it. My heart was heavy that morning. And the odor seemed to have a line with a hook in my heart, drawing me deeper into a pit of depression as I reflected on my life. It was as if no one really knew or cared about what I was going through. And here I was with a child whom I loved very much. A child that I was responsible for, to look after, provide for, and watch over. All the while, deep in my broken heart, and mixed-up state of mind, I felt I needed someone to care for me.

I felt like God was far from me and maybe even forgotten me. Yet and still, I ironed and continued to cry out to Him. Never opening my mouth, in silence, I cried out. "Where are you God? You seem so far away. I need to hear from You." I continued to cry out to Him desperately as if my cries were somehow searching for Him and would find Him. Also, in my mind, I had become consumed and drawn deeper into a pit of depression, not being aware of anything else going on around me.

Suddenly, a sweet-smelling aroma filled the room. The aroma was so sweet, pleasant and strong. It caught my attention so much so, it caused me to turn around to see where it was coming from; simultaneously causing me to forget about all that I was going through. It seems to have the opposite effect of the unpleasant odor I had experienced from the hot iron pressing down on the skirt. It was as if the Sweet aroma also had a line and hook in me, drawing me out of the pit. It was captivating!

As I turned to see what was causing the aroma, there was my daughter standing there at the sink. She was getting a drink of water. I stood there, admiring her perfectly framed body. She was all dressed up. So precious in my sight, and so innocent. I just stood there watching her, adoring her, realizing how much I loved her. Also realizing how much she needed me. I am her mother, obligated to take care of her. I could or would never leave her. Everything would be alright, I thought as I began to regain confidence. And at the same time, realizing my Heavenly Father was saying the same thing to me.

How often, when going through trials or tribulation, we forget how much He loves us. He will take care of us. He said that He would never leave us nor forsake us *(Hebrews 13:5)*. Even when we don't realize it, He is watching over us, loving us, preparing, and working things out for us. Our very prayers are like a sweet-smelling aroma *(Revelations 5:8)* that causes Him to look on us. They catch His attention *(1Peter 3:12)*. He is always there watching over us, waiting for us to cry out to Him. Even when we don't realize it, He is watching us even when our backs are towards Him.

A Word of Wisdom

Although sometimes we feel all alone,

and in our lives, it seems all hope is gone.

We must take time to see what we have,

which in our heart we hold so dear.

Then we can clearly see,

and know that the Lord is always near.

Carrying Our Pain

"Cast all your anxiety on him because he cares for you."
(1Peter 5:7 NIV)

"Brothers and sisters, I do not consider myself yet to have taken
hold of it. But one thing I do: Forgetting what is behind and
straining toward what is ahead, I press on toward the goal to
win the prize for which God has called me heavenward in Christ
Jesus."
(Philippians 3:13-14 NIV)

My grandson loved playing on the monkey bars. He was five years old and in kindergarten. Not being very strong, his goal was to cross from one side to the other without falling off. Each day he would tell me how he practiced during recess. He would explain with excitement and enthusiasm how he was able to go further without falling off. And by his achievements, I knew that he was building muscle and getting stronger.

Well, with all his practicing, he developed a blister in the palm of his hand. And one day, while persevering to reach his goal, he caused the blister to tear. When I picked him up from school, he held his injured hand cupped close to his chest, as if it were in a sling. As he got closer to me, I noticed that he also had a wet paper towel covering the torn blister. The rest of the day, I watched him as he held his hand in front of him as if he was actually carrying the pain. He was continually focusing on it, keeping his attention on it.

I tried to comfort him. I put ointment on it and covered it with a bandage, which he took off because he couldn't see it. I tried everything I could to get his mind off the wound, hoping he would forget about it and not focus on the pain. I told him, "Be a big boy. It will be okay. We all got those when we were children. In time, it will heal. And when it does, your hand will be a little tougher. And it won't tear as easily next time." But no matter what I said or did to try and make it better, he wasn't hearing it. He didn't want to forget about it. Every now and then, he would come running into the room where I was and with his hand extended out in front of him screaming, "It hurts, it hurts!" He wanted to let me know he was hurting and everyone else around that he was hurting. For the rest of the evening, he held on to that pain until he went to bed. Still holding his hand in front of him as if he was afraid that he would lose it sometime in the night. I stood there looking at him with his injured hand laying there, with his palm towards his face. It was as if, although he was asleep, he was still carrying the pain through the night over into the next morning. Anticipating to continue to focus on the injury and carry the pain throughout the next day.

As I reflected on the tiring incident, I began to become aware of how we so often portray the same characteristics of my five-year-old grandson. How often we hold our disappointments, hurts, and woes in life before us, always looking at them. We talk about them, focusing on them being consumed by them until they control our very actions, not wanting to forget about them and wanting everyone else to remember them.

And the Lord is trying to tell us, "Stop focusing on it. It will be okay." Trying to comfort us and heal us from it *(1Peter 5:7)*. But still, we carry it around always before us until it paralyzes us in that moment, hindering us from reaching our goals. We should always listen to the Father, hear His words, letting them be to our pain as the balm of Gilead. We should allow Him to heal us, letting go of our past pain, disappointments, failures and woes in this life *(Philippians 3:13-14)*. Then we will be able to forget the past, live more abundant in the present and focus more on and move towards our future. This will bring us to the realization of: The weeping that is caused by our pain today is the certainty of our joy of the victory for tomorrow.

A Word of Wisdom

We shall have sorrows, disappointments, and woes

but if without hesitation we would let them go,

and hear the words of our Heavenly Father

that comforts, heals and nurtures

we would understand, (although painful as it may be),

our present situation doesn't determine our future.

The Eagle and the Dove

"Jesus answered, 'I am the way, the truth, and the life: No one comes to the Father, except through me." (John 14:6 NIV)

"And I will ask the Father, and he will give you another advocate to help you and be with you forever." (John 14:16 NIV)

It was hot! The flowers were wilted from the hot sun bearing down on them. And the same effect the sun was having on the flowers, I felt like the trial I was going through was having the same effect on me. I had just suffered the death of my daughter, my only child, and inherited my grandson, who was a one-year-old.

I was lonely, broken and cried out desperately to God for comfort and strength, to care for my grandson and three other children. My niece and her husband were in another town in the hospital with their premature baby and had been there for weeks. They were in the military and I was in their home caring for their three children. My grandson and I had traveled from our home, which was about four hours away, and I didn't know anyone else on the base. It was a chore caring for four children being that I was used to caring for only one. There wasn't much time for quiet time or anything else, so I thought.

But this day, my grandson was down for a nap, and the other children were in school. So I figured that I would get as much done as I could while I had the chance. I began going through the house, gathering all the laundry from the bedrooms. Three of the bedrooms were on one side of the house, and the master bedroom was on the other side. The sitting room was between the master bedroom and the other three bedrooms. So I had to pass the front door to get to the master bedroom from the other bedrooms.

With it being hot, I had the front door opened and had a good view of the front yard through the glass storm door. As I passed the front door, I saw what appeared to be a small statue sitting in the yard right in front of the porch, directly in front of the door. "Who put that there?" I asked myself as I approached the door to get a better look. To my surprise, it wasn't a statue after all. It was an eagle, and it had a dove clinched by the neck between its beaks as if it were choking it out. It sat there for a few seconds looking directly at me as if it wanted to be sure that I was certain of what I was seeing. Then suddenly, it took off soaring in the air, leaving me with my thoughts boggling my mind.

A bird eating a bird? What a strange thing to see, I thought. Something seemed very wrong with that picture to me. But at the same time, I realized that it was an answer to my cry.

You see, the eagle is often used as a symbol of a born-again believer, and the dove is often used as a symbol of the Holy Spirit. And at that very moment, they both were being used to relay a message to me.

While I cried out to God for what I needed, I didn't take the time to listen or be still long enough for Him to do what I was asking Him to do. I cried out to Him while I allowed myself to become lost in grief, caring for everyone and everything else until I had choked the very one out that I needed the most.

So often, we become so caught up in the busyness and cares of this world until we leave very little or no time at all for much-needed healing from God. We cry out to Him with our complaints and struggles while He's trying to minister to us and answer our cries. But during our busyness and crying out, we choke Him out.

We must remember to make time to sit at His feet and listen for the answer to our cries (John 14:16). When going through times, we must sit in His presence and invite the Holy Spirit in so He can calm our weary souls. We cry out to Him and choke out the very one He sent to us as the comforter *(John 14:6)* and there is something wrong with that picture.

A Word of Wisdom

Lord help us not to be consumed

with the cares of this world

when in our lives all around us busyness swirl.

And when we cry to the Father in heaven,

who looks down in love,

remind us to also sit quietly

And listen to the one whom You

sent from above.

That we don't portray the picture

of the eagle and the dove.

Seeking His Face

"My heart says of you, 'Seek his face!' Your face, LORD, I will seek." (Psalms 27:8 NIV)

"And without faith it is impossible to please God, because anyone who comes to him must believe that he exists and that he rewards those who earnestly seek him." (Hebrews 11:6 NIV)

I was in my early twenties and a newlywed. My husband had enlisted into the military and was returning home from basic training. My mother-in-law, her husband, and I had traveled to another town to pick him up from the airport.

It had been a long wait, the two months or so he had been gone. And the ride to the airport from our hometown made it seem even longer as I anticipated seeing his face.

We finally arrived at the airport, and the plane had landed. As the passengers poured through the door, I searched the crowd for his face. When I saw him, the excitement became so overwhelming that I began to leap slightly while clapping my hands saying, "There he is, there he is!" I was so glad to see him knowing we would be able to enjoy each other, talking and spend valuable time alone.

On the ride home, he told me he brought me gifts. But that didn't matter at the time because I knew the best gift he could have given me, himself. And the most important thing was that I was in his presence again.

Well, years passed, I'm born again, and my life is different now. I no longer have that husband, but that's another story. So here I am alone, thinking back over my life, wondering how I got there. As I thought, that airport moment came to mind. I began to reminisce on how happy I was to see him; how I search the crowd anxiously. And at that moment, I realized that the Lord desired the same response when it came to me seeking His face and being in His presence *(Psalms 27:8).*

Often in our prayer and meditation time, we are asking for things or complaining so much. With our heads bowed down to the ground and our eyes closed, we don't take time to look through the crowd of our wants, needs, and complaints to seek His face. Do we seek His face diligently? *(Hebrews 11:6)* Do we honestly seek His presence?

We must make seeking His face and being in His presence a priority in our lives. We must not seek His hands, that if we stood face to face with Him in a crowd, we probably wouldn't recognize who He was. If God's people would make seeking the master's face become a priority in their lives, we would see that there is no greater gift we could ever receive than to be in the presence of the Lord.

A Word of Wisdom

Although the gifts from our Father are great,

when served to us from His hands

On a spiritual plate

We must never allow them in our life

to take first place

But always remember

the greatest gift is to be able to seek His face.

The Evergreen Tree

*"But you are a chosen people, a royal priesthood, a holy nation,
God's special possession, that you may declare the praises of him
who called you out of darkness into his wonderful light."*
(1 Peter 2:9 NIV)

In the spring, the trees are blooming. The grass is turning
green, birds are chirping, the sun is shining and a lot of the
time showers of rain are falling! This has always been my
favorite time of the year. I would sit on my front porch and watch
life unfolding right before my eyes. As I sat there enjoying the
beauty of it all, the wind began to blow just enough to cause the
branches on the trees to move about. I began to focus on the trees
as far as I could see. Although there were different kinds of trees,
they all appeared to be the same from a distance. Except for the
one that sat amid a group of trees in the neighbor's yard. Of
course, it caught my eye and stole my focus from all the other
trees.

This tree was quite different than the other trees. It was some type
of evergreen tree. It stood straight up, and the narrow towering
was way above all the others. It appeared to have been perfectly
pruned. And its color was a deeper and richer green than the
other trees. As the wind blew, the branches of the other trees
moved about in all different directions, appearing to change
shapes with the force of the wind. But the evergreen tree stood

straight up, swaying slightly at the top, while the rest of it stood strong against the wind. The branches would all move in harmony, as one, not changing its shape.

From that day on, I was always aware of that tree. Whether I was close or a few blocks away, it stood out. It was more noticeable than all the other trees. With this experience, I came to understand that this was how God wants His people to be, like that evergreen tree. He wants us to stand out in the crowd. We are not to be like the world. We are to be different from the world, although in the midst of it. We are to allow Him to take away all the things that will keep us from being different from the world, allowing Him to change us that we may appear perfectly pruned. We are to be a peculiar people *(1 Peter 2:9)*. When our lives are being viewed from any perspective, we should stand out in the crowd. Though the wind may blow, and the storms come, we should stand strong. We should not change or handle things the way the world does. But we are to be the opposite of the world in every situation. We should be so different until there is evidence that Christ lives in us.

A Word of Wisdom

Though the storms come, and the winds blow,

we should stand strong so that the world will know

we are peculiar creatures being recreated by the Father.

Being perfectly molded, made, shaped, and

born again into a state that will not falter.

The Perfect Example

"You call me 'Teacher' and 'Lord,' and rightly so, for that is what I am. Now that I, your Lord and Teacher, have washed your feet, you also should wash one another's feet. I have set you an example that you should do as I have done to you. Very truly I tell you, no servant is greater than his mater, nor is a messenger greater than the one who sent him."
(John 13:13-16 NIV)

"To this you were called, because Christ suffered for you, leaving you an example, that you should follow his steps."
(1Peter 2:21 NIV)

My youngest sister was getting married. She had given me the honor of being in charge of decorating. We had a very tight budget to work with. So I decided I would use some items from the homes of our family to make this occasion as grand as possible.

I decided to use artificial trees adorned with white flowers on either side of the altar. I owned one of the trees. It stood about six feet high and had rich dark green foliage from about midway to the top of the trunk.

Showing my tree as an example, I asked throughout the family, hoping someone had another one. If not identical, so similar that you wouldn't be able to tell much difference between the two.

Well, the day for decorating had arrived. We met at the church with all the decorations and all the trees everyone had brought for us to select from.

Everything seemed to be going as planned, except for the trees we were to use at the altar. It surprised me how, although I used my tree as an example, all the other trees brought to the church were nothing like it. One of the trees was about five feet tall, with pale green leaves covering most of the trunk. The other two were not trees at all. They were two four-foot artificial bamboo plants. It made me wonder if anyone had paid any attention to the example, I had given them at all.

While looking over all the artificial plants wondering what I would do, my mind took a turn towards God's people.

While living a Christian life, fellowshipping and communicating with other believers, there is so much difference among us. Sometimes in many ways there appears to be little or no likeness at all.

There are a lot of people called Christians. But whom or what are we using as an example? Mankind (people we so easily call our mentors)? Do we have our own idea of what a Christian should be (self-righteousness)?

Or do we look to the example that has been given us *(John 13:13-16) (1Peter 2:21),* which we are to model our lives after. Remember, there is no greater example than the Perfect Example, Jesus Christ!

A Word of Wisdom

We must be careful who we choose to reflect.

Lest in our choosing we forget the one who lived His life perfect.

For His word says: we shall be like Him, and His word is true

So much so that one wouldn't be able to tell much difference

between the two. So let us model our life after Jesus Christ.

After all, we wouldn't want to call just any example

CHRIST LIKE.

A Hard Heart

"Jesus answered her, 'If you knew the gift of God, and who it is that asks you for a drink, you would have asked of him and he would have given you living water.' 'Sir,' the woman said, 'you have nothing to draw with and the well is deep, Where can you get this living water? Are you greater than our father Jacob, who gave us the well and drank from it himself, as did also his sons and his livestock?' Jesus answered, 'Everyone who drinks this water will be thirsty again, but whoever drinks the water I give them will never thirst. Indeed, the water I give them will become in them a spring of water welling up to eternal life.'
(John 4:10-14 NIV)

'Then the master told his servant, 'Go out to the roads and county lanes and compel them to come in, so that my house will be full.'
(Luke 14:23 NIV)

Planting flowers and working in gardens is one of my passions. It's a great time for me to communicate with God and to meditate on Him and His word. It's a time for asking questions and listening for answers.

Every year I have to clear the ground of blown-in debris and the dead plants from the previous year. While pulling up plants from the previous year, some of the seed would fall to the ground. After clearing the ground, I can hardly wait to cultivate the soil, preparing the soil to receive the seed I am to plant and the seed from the previous year.

The cultivating was going smooth at first. Although I was working in the same garden, some sections were a little harder. And as I progressed in cultivating, I found out that some areas were just too hard. So, I flooded the almost rock-hard ground with water and waited for it to soak in to soften the soil. This makes the ground so much easier to cultivate.

While waiting for the dry, thirsty ground to soak up the water, I sat on the front stoop. As I sat there, I began to think about the process that took place when the water was applied to the hard-dry ground. As I meditated, even more, another process began to take place in my mind.

I began to see how we as Christians are working sowing and planting seed in the hearts of unbelievers. Some hearts are soft, easily accepting seed. While some hearts are hard and stone-like, making it almost impossible to receive the seed that needs to be planted.

But what if we used the same application to the heart as we do to the garden? What if we apply the living water *(John 4:10-14)*, the word of God, repeatedly until that hard heart soaks it up being made ready and able to receive seed.

We should treat every hard heart as if it were soil in a flower garden and not give up so easily when hearts seem too hard to cultivate. We should apply that living water (the word of God) every chance we get until it soaks in. Then the hard heart may become soft enough to cultivate and receive the seed that is so desperately needed to be planted—compelling them to come *(Luke 14:23)*.

A Word of Wisdom

While sowing seeds in Gods precious garden

remember that some hearts, we are to pardon.

For we know on hard hearts, some of the seeds may fall

But we must remember, God gave His Son for all.

So, let us not be deceived in what God wishes to achieve,

if we just keep applying the living water and believe.

In time, the seed, the heart will receive.

The Cocoon

"But I am a worm and not a man, scorned by everyone, despises
by the people." (Psalms 22:6 NIV)

Answer me quickly, Lord: my spirit fails. Do not hide your face
from me or I will be like those who go down to the pit. Let the
morning bring me word of your unfailing love, for I have put my
trust in you. Show me the way I should go, for to you I entrust
my life. Rescue me from my enemies, Lord, for I hide myself in
you. Teach me to do your will, for you are my God: may your
good Spirit lead me on level ground. For your name's sake, Lord,
preserve my life; in your righteousness, bring me out of trouble."
(Psalms 143:7-11 NIV)

"Therefore, if anyone is in Christ, the new creation has come:
The old has gone, the new is here!"
(2 Corinthians 5:17 NIV)

Have you ever considered the cocoon? It's really not that
pleasant to look at. It can be ugly in one way and beautiful in
another way. The cocoon signifies the end of one way of life
and, at the same time, the beginning of a new way of life.

As I sat on my mother's front porch one afternoon, considering
the cocoon, my mind was taken back to before it became a
cocoon. It was a caterpillar, a worm.

I thought about how the worm could only crawl on its belly. It was so limited. It was at its lowest state of life. The caterpillar couldn't see any further than its environment. It was very vulnerable to its prey.

But the worm has an advantage that very few if any other creature has.

You see, at the right season, the worm somehow begins to be drawn upward. And after reaching a certain level, it begins to separate itself from the world. And a change begins to take place, metamorphosis. A mystery, as though it enters a type of womb again being formed into a new creature.

Nothing like it was before, born again, being able to exceed the life of limitations it was bound by before. It excels into new heights and explores new territory, now living way above the means of a worm or caterpillar. It has become a new creation, indeed. It has become a butterfly.

The beauty of the new creature surpasses the old so until there is no comparison.

And while I thought on these things, I began to see a parallel, a likeness of how we as Christians are changed. How we were once in the lowest state of life. You see, we were as worms *(Psalms 22:6)*, limited to and bound by sin, only able to operate in a limited environment, the natural. Then in due season, we are drawn upward in a spiritual sense to Christ (to things above). He separates us and begins a work in us that others cannot yet see *(Psalms 143:7-11)*. It is hidden from the natural eye. It is hidden in the womb of our hearts. A mystery, a new creation takes place. We too, become born again.

We are then able to experience a new life, explore new territory and excel into new heights. And when considering the old and the new life, there is no comparison.

Like the worm that surpasses its former state, we too, transcend our former state of being. We are no longer just natural, but supernatural. We become a new creation in Christ Jesus *(2 Corinthians 5:17)*.

A Word of Wisdom

Consider the cocoon, for it tells a story

And hidden in it is a covert example of God's Glory

Because if we parallel the worm and man

we will understand when Jesus said

"You must be born again."

The Rocking Chair

"And provide for those who grieve in Zion- to bestow on them a crown of beauty instead of ashes, the oil of joy instead of mourning, and a garment of praise instead of a spirit of despair. They will be called oaks of righteousness, a planting of the Lord for the display of his splendor." (Isaiah 61:3 NIV)

In August 2001, I suffered a great tragedy. I lost my only child. The previous nine or ten years of my life had already been like a kite spiraling downward out of control. So the death of my daughter was as though I had hit rock bottom. I felt that it was the end of my shattered, mixed-up life. I felt I was done. Nothing in my life seemed to matter or make since anymore. I felt I was just existing, going through the motions of life, but feeling all washed out and used up. Put out in the wasteland of life left to die.

Although I was still active in the Church, I felt it was more of a physical than spiritual participation.

I was the church decorator at the time. And some of the other members and I were decorating for the Pastor's appreciation day. This would always require several trips to the church leading up to that day.

This particular day I was unloading some materials at the back of the church. I noticed an old rocking chair sitting in the ally by the dumpster. It caught my eye. Every trip after that, the old worn-out rocking chair seem to draw my attention. It was as if it were calling out to me in some phenomenal way. It was as if the old chair was pleading to me to not leave it there.

So, one day I loaded up the old chair and took it home with me. I decided to try and upholster it. It was still of some use. It just needed some work to show it still had some worth. It wasn't so far gone until it needed to be thrown away. I was sure I could work with it and make it look new again.

As I began to rip away the old fabric and strip it down to the frame, a spiritual lesson began to unfold. A revelation of how the Lord takes our old life and make it new again. When it seems all hope for us is gone if we would just cry out. Cry out to the one who can make a difference in our lives. Cry out to the one who can make beauty from ashes *(Isaiah 61:3)*. We would find out that there is hope. We would come to know that we are not worthless. But to the Savior, we are treasures waiting and longing to be revealed.

I took that old chair and restored it, and it is like new again. When no one else could see the worth of that old chair, I somehow did.

With the help of the Holy Spirit, I learned a lesson that changed my perspective on life.

You see, God would never throw away anyone or anything of value when no one else can see your worth. If you feel your life is over and all hope is gone. God hears your cry. Cry out to Him and let Him restore your life today.

A Word of Wisdom

When it seems you are all alone

and you feel all hope is gone.

Just cry out to the one who cares,

and remember the old rocking chair.

For our worth extends beyond our life.

Because we are worth the life of Christ.

A Good Work

"Being confident of this, that he who began a good work in you will carry it on to completion until the day of Christ Jesus."
(Philippians 1: 6 NIV)

In the early to late 90's I was caring for my mother-in-law, who had cancer. We lived in a very small agricultural town. So whenever she had a doctor's appointment or was admitted into the hospital, we would have to drive about an hour and a half to another town. I would also stay with her whenever she was admitted.

Seeing the need for me to be available, I wouldn't commit to a career or a job. So I laid my life aside for a while.

With me not having a steady income, when time permitted, I worked in the cotton fields as a hired hand-chopping weeds.

Some of the fields were a mile or more wide, and the individual rows were just as much in length.

I remember while working one day, the sun seemed extra hot, and the heat was bearing down hard on me. The field was full of weeds that stood so tall. From a distance, they appeared to be small trees.

It was after lunch, and we had hoed only about one-third of the field. "Give me strength," I whispered while looking over the portion of the field we had not yet hoed. It was a mess. The weeds were so thick I couldn't even see the cotton as I stood there feeling exhausted, searching to see the end of the field. At that time, it became overwhelming. It gave me a sense of hopelessness. I began to wonder if I would be able to go on. But when I looked back over the portion of the field, we had hoed, it was a picture of beauty.

It appeared neat, all cleaned up. The cotton stood swaying slightly and seemed to shimmer from the reflection of the sunlight. There wasn't a weed in sight.

Although I was tired, the beauty of it seemed to refresh me, giving me the strength to go on.

As I continued to work and meditate on what I had just experienced, I was reminded of how I would so often feel about my life as a Christian. I felt so undone. There were so many wrongs still in my life. There were still so many changes that needed to be made. There were so many old ways still towering over me that hid the beauty of what God created me to be. At times it would become overwhelming. I would have a sense of hopelessness of never becoming what God wanted me to be.

This experience reminded me of how far He had already brought me. Even though I wasn't totally what He wanted me to be, I knew He had begun to wash and change me. He had taken some of my old ugly ways out of me.

I believe the experience was His way of encouraging me and reminding me that He has begun a good work in me and that He will perform it until the day of the return of Jesus Christ *(Philippians 1: 6).*

A Word of Wisdom

When we get in this journey we are on,

And can't see the right He has done in our life

Because we focus more on the wrong.

Let us reflect on where He has brought us from.

For it's not by power, but by His spirit we have come

So trust that the one who have begun the good work,

Will be sure to see that it gets done.

The Purchase

"For you know that it was not with perishable things such as silver or gold that you were redeemed from the empty way of life handed down to you from your ancestors, but with the precious blood of Christ, a lamb without blemish or defect, He was chosen before the creation of the world, but was revealed in these last times for your sake." (1Peter 1:18-19 NIV)

"The Lord makes firm the steps of the one who delights in him." (Psalm 37:23 NIV)

"You were bought at a price; do not become slaves of human beings." (1 Corinthians 7:23 NIV)

I inherited my grandson after the passing away of my daughter. He was a year old and very strong-willed. We lived in an apartment that I had renovated. Everything was like new. I had made it a home where we could comfortably live. It was a place where I could display all the things that I had purchased, which was in safari style.

I had purchased three ceramic giraffes and placed them inside the entertainment center behind a glass door, which I thought was the perfect place for them at the time.

After living in the apartment for some time, I was ready for a change. So, while cleaning the house one day, I decided to change some of the placements of the decor. I decided I would place the giraffes on the coffee table in a better view. I finished cleaning the room and went into the bedroom to clean it.

The phone rang, and I returned to the front room to answer it. Looking around the room while engaged in my conversation on the phone, I felt satisfied with the work I had done. Everything looked good in its new place. Change was good. It gave me a sense of freshness until my eyes met the coffee table. The giraffes were not there, they were back in the entertainment center behind the glass door. That's funny I thought I placed them on the coffee table, I said to myself. But without a second thought, I placed them on the coffee table. I finished my phone conversation and returned to the bedroom to continue cleaning.

Time passed, the bedroom was clean, and I decided to take a break so my grandson and I could have a snack. With my grandson already eating his snack in the kitchen, I decided I would have mine in the front room so that I could watch a little television. When I sat down, I noticed the giraffes were back in the entertainment center behind the glass door. This is crazy. I know for sure I placed them on the coffee table, I thought to myself. So again, I placed them on the coffee table and sat down to eat my snack and watch television, feeling a little spooked.

A few minutes later, my grandson came into the front room, noticing the giraffes on the coffee table. He runs and opens the glass door to the entertainment center, places the giraffes back into it, and closed the door. He then turns toward me shaking his little finger at me, speaking in an incomprehensible language (as if he were scolding me). He then turned and ran out of the room.

I sat there, stunned. I couldn't believe what I had just witnessed. I felt my authority had just been violated by a one-year-old.

I guess he felt that he had just as much authority in the house as I did. He had to have felt that everything in the house was just as much his as it was mine. Yes, he must have felt that he had just as much ownership of the things I had purchased as I did.

He didn't want the giraffes placed anywhere else. In his little childlike mind, he didn't understand change. And with his actions, he showed me he didn't want things to change. I guess he figured that's where they had been since they were brought into the house, and that's where they were to stay.

When I came to myself, I called him back into the room and told him (as silly as it may have seemed at the time), "I don't want them there anymore, I bought them, and I want them on the coffee table now."

As I placed the giraffes again on the coffee table while still scolding my grandson about overriding my authority, my mind began to take a turn. The Holy Spirit began to relate to me a similar lesson. He began to show me how so many leaders and other believers violate the authority of the purchaser of His property.

You see, God purchased his people with His son's blood *(1Peter 1:18-19)*. He suffered and died to redeem us to the Father. No one else paid the price for us. Therefore no one else has the right to claim ownership over lives. And when He redeemed us, He places us where He will as long as He will. And when He moves us, He moves us for His purpose and His plan. The steps of a good man are ordered by the Lord *(Psalms 37:23)*. No one has the right to be offended by His actions. It's His house, and He can set it up any way He pleases. He can change things however He pleases. He can use whoever, however, and wherever he pleases.

If we as God's children would remember who did the purchasing and not take ownership over His purchase. We would be able to freely serve Him. And know that whether He moves us to a different position or a different house, that the steps of a good man are ordered by the Lord, let us as children of God remember not to let our will override His will. He paid the price. It's His house and His plan for every person that He purchased. For we were bought with a price. We are not to be servants to please man, but Christ *(1 Corinthians 7:23)*.

A Word of Wisdom

Let us as children of God remember,

God's will we are not to override.

It's His purchase, His house, His plan,

Because He paid the price.

The Renovation

"Do not judge, or you too will be judged. For in the same way you judge others, you will be judged, and with the measure you use, it will be measured to you. 'Why do you look at the speck of sawdust in your brother's eye and pay no attention to the plank in your own eye? How can you say to your brother, 'Let me take the speck out of your eye,' when all the time there is a plank in your own eye?' (Matthew 7:1-4 NIV)

Critics can be as bad as locust eating away at a beautiful field of crop. And currently in my life, they were attacking my life from every side (the critics, that is). This caused me to begin to question my confidence as a Christian. It also begins to send me into a deep depression. All I wanted to do was to please God and be led by the Holy Spirit. And allow Him to remake me that I might become more like Jesus.

But it seems the more I tried (as hard as it was at the time), the more critical people seemed to be towards me. So, I began to cry out to God, asking, what's wrong with me? Is it me, Lord? Am I that messed up to where no one can see the Christ in me? This became my cry over and over again.

Then one Sunday, while returning home from worship service, He answered me in the most surprising way.

You see, at the time, I had rented a house that had been almost fully renovated on the inside, all except the garage and, of course, the outside of the house. The house was beautiful on the inside. There were shiny hardwood floors in every room except the kitchen and bathroom which had been done with large ceramic tiles. Extra-large windows were across the front of the house that allowed lots of sunlight in, and new windows throughout the rest of the house. There were new cabinets in the kitchen. The walls were painted throughout the house in different pastel colors. This gave each room a feeling of warmth as though the owner had put his character in the house. There had been a lot of work done, although it was not yet finished.

The outside was not yet painted. You could still see where the owner had replaced the windows and patched holes with new stucco. From the outside, it appeared to be the oldest and ugliest house on the block.

As I was pulling into the driveway of my home, it all began to unfold—a revelation. As I looked at the house, I realized I was being viewed the same way many people were viewing my home. You see, no one knew how it looked on the inside. They only judged what they could see on the outside *(Matthew 7:1-4)*. No one knew the beauty and value of the house. Only the one who did the renovation, the one who lived in the house, and the one who owned the house. Wow! What excitement rushed through me. I knew at that moment the Lord had heard my cry and answered me.

He was showing me that He was recreating me on the inside. He was doing a work in me that man could not yet see. He had changed my heart. I was being judged as the old person and not by the beauty God had placed on the inside of me.

When I realized this, it didn't matter what the critics said anymore. Their opinion didn't have the same effect on me as before. As long as the owner (God the Father), the renovator (the Holy Spirit), the tenant (Jesus) who lives inside of me, and me (the house), are aware of the changes made in me. I have a joy that the critics can never take away from me.

A Word of Wisdom

When life's critics try and cut you down,

and sometimes their words make you feel

that your old ways have you bound.

Just remember they are unable,

to see the change inside of you.

and that their actions reflect,

that they still need work done too.

The Potter and The Clay

"Yet you, Lord, are our Father. We are the clay, you are the potter; we are all the work of your hand." (Isaiah 64:8 NIV)

"This is the word that came to Jeremiah from the LORD: 'Go down to the potter's house, and there I will give you my message." So I went down to the potter's house, and I saw him working at the wheel, But the pot he was shaping from the clay was marred in his hands; so the potter formed it into another pot, shaping it as seemed best to him. Then the word of the Lord came to me. He said, 'Can I not do with you, Israel, as this potter does?' declares the Lord. "Like clay in the hand of the potter, so are you in my hand, Israel. (Jeremiah 18:1-6 NIV)

"I baptize you with water for repentance. But after me comes one who is more powerful than I, whose sandals I am not worthy to carry. He will baptize you with the Holy Spirit and fire." (Matthew 3:11 NIV)

"Nevertheless, God's solid foundation stands firm, sealed with this inscription: 'The Lord knows those who are his,' and, 'Everyone who confesses the name of the Lord must turn away from wickedness.' In a large house there are articles not only of gold and silver, but also of wood and clay; some are for special purposes and some for common use. Those who cleanse themselves from the latter will be instruments for special

purposes, made holy, useful to the Master and prepared to do
any good work. Flee the evil desires of youth and pursue
righteousness, faith, love and peace, along with those who call
on the Lord out of a pure heart." (2 Timothy 2:19-22 NIV)

It's amazing how a potter (one who makes earthen pots) can take clay and form beautiful vessels. The extent one would take to create one pot is surprising. There is a lot of work that goes into making pottery. It's a creative process. One would have to know what he is working toward before beginning the process of creating it. The potter would already have in his mind what the finished product would be. The potter would first have to purchase the clay, take it to the place where all the necessary equipment is to do his work, and the process begins.

Separating, crushing, grinding, and breaking down the clay sometimes to mere dust. Then it is mixed with water to make the clay easily moldable. Thoroughly wet, the clay can be molded into anything. It depends on the potter. After the clay is the right consistency, it is placed on a wheel. It must be in the center of the wheel, held and molded by the potter. If not it could easily be slung off and damaged because the wheel spins so fast.

While working with the clay on the wheel, the potter continually adds water while molding and shaping the clay. This process goes on until the desired vessel is formed by the potter's own hands.

Although the vessel has been formed into the desired shape, it is still too soft for use. The potter then takes the shaped vessel (handling it very carefully to avoid any damage) and places it into the kiln.

The kiln is a large oven with intense heat that purifies the clay turning the color of the clay from gray to white. It makes the vessel able to take a little more pressure than the former state.

The vessel is now ready to be sanded and painted or given whatever character or design the potter desires. The potter is now able to make it his own, making it beautiful, his masterpiece. It has been known that a master potter puts his signature on his product, giving it an identity. Still, with all this work done, the vessel stands not ready for use. The vessel has to be fired in the kiln again with more intense heat. But before it is, the potter puts a finish over all his design and signature he has placed on the vessel. When fired, the finish creates a protective coat and seals all the work that the potter has done to the vessel.

After firing, the vessel is now ready for use. It can be filled. It can now hold whatever the potter wishes to place in it. It can be used for people to eat and drink from. It can be used for whatever it was created for.

Isn't this a similar process the Heavenly Father takes with His children?

(Isaiah 64:8) says, "But now, O Lord, thou art our Father; and we are the clay, and thou our potter; and we all are the work of thy hands."

(Jeremiah 18:1-6) speaks of how God uses the potter and the clay to illustrate the creative process between Him and His people.

Let's take a look at it. Before we accept Jesus Christ as our Lord and Savior, we are like clay laying waste in some desert place. We are of no specific use, no purpose, just basically existing, just part of a clay pile.

Then the Lord finds us. The Molder, the Maker, Creator, the Master Craftsman, the Lord, the Potter.

We are broken away from a familiar place, taken out of the world to be taken in. We enter the kingdom of God, into the Potter's house. We enter the workplace into His presence, a place where all the necessary elements are to be made a vessel. This is where the process begins.

Crushing, grinding breaking down, and away from the old state of life in preparation for the Potter to begin giving us new life.

Then comes the mixing with water (the word) the living water—hearing God's word over and over again, being purged immersed until our hearts are softened. We are now able to be molded into whatever vessel the Father desires us to be.

I remember watching a documentary on television about the potter and the clay. I watched the potter molding the clay on the wheel, steadily adding water while shaping the clay. It appeared at times that the hands of the potter would go inside of the clay or that the clay would slightly cover the potter's hands as if they were becoming one. And the potter would steady keep his hands on the clay, never letting go.

This is how the Heavenly Father is with his children. He will never let us go. In the process of molding and shaping us, making us into beautiful vessels, He will never let go.

Then comes the purification, where we are purified, cleansed. Our old ways are taken away. Like the first firing in the kiln. We have been changed from an old state of being to a new state of being. We become a vessel but not quite ready for use.

The Father begins to give us character, a new way of life, a new heart and mind. He imparts in us some of who He is, His character. But back into the fire, we go, for He said He would baptize us with fire *(Matthew 3:11)*. This creates a shield of faith.

Then we are ready for use. We are ready to be filled with The Holy Spirit, so we can become vessels of honor to the one who created us *(2 Timothy 2:19-22)*.

A Word of Wisdom

If you feel you have no worth.

If you are lost and can't find your way.

If you feel you have no purpose and your life lay waste,

Only existing from day to day.

Remember what the Father told Jeremiah,

"Arise go down to the potter's house..."and there stay.

For its there you will begin to experience

the wonderful creative process of the potter and the

clay. And by the way He did purchase the clay.

But He paid the ultimate price, a blood sacrifice, He gave His life.

Justified

"After he has suffered, he will see the light and be satisfied; by his knowledge my righteous servant will justify many, and he will bear their iniquities." (Isaiah 53:11 NIV)

I have a brother who has been diagnosed as being mentally ill. At one time, he would always get in trouble. With him being in the condition that he was in, people would always take advantage of him. This time two young women sold him a car that was not theirs. The car wasn't registered or insured. And my brother didn't even have a license to drive.

Wow! He was so excited! He thought he could drive around and listen to music and be cool like a lot of the other guys he knew. He felt like he was finally in the mix. He didn't think about or realize what was really going on. He didn't realize he was breaking the law in more ways than one. But he couldn't help himself. He was just happy that he had bought a car and had done it with his own money. So he felt it was alright.

Well, while taking a cruise one day, he was pulled over by the police. There he was driving a stolen vehicle, with no license, no registration and no insurance. So he went to jail.

After sitting in jail for a long period of time while our family did everything in our power to plead his case, we contacted judges and his public defender over and over again, trying to let them know his condition in hopes that he would be released. But nothing changed. He still sat in jail, waiting for his court day to arrive.

Finally, the day arrived for him to appear in court. And a lot of our family was there on his behalf.

The public defender pleaded his case. He explained to the judge how my brother was a severe schizophrenic. He explained how my brother was not competent enough to stand trial and never would be.

The judge showing mercy, threw out all charges against him and my brother walked out of the courtroom that day a free man.

As I witnessed the event that day, I realized it was an illustration of what God the Father and The Son did for us. We are justified through Christ *(Isaiah 53:11)*.

When we accept Jesus as our Lord and Savior, all our sin is forgiven. It's wiped away.

We could never be competent enough to stand before the righteous judge (God The Father). But because Jesus died in our place and plead our case, we can walk out of bondage free today just if we had never sinned.

A Word of Wisdom

The human race is evil in our ways.

So thank you Father for applying your grace.

My sin has been forgiven, never to be brought before me again.

Because of what Your son Jesus did, I'm JUST-IF-IED never sinned.

The Special China Set

"He told them, 'The harvest is plentiful, but the workers are few. Ask the Lord of the harvest, therefore, to send out workers into his harvest field." (Luke 10:2 NIV)

"I pray that out of his glorious riches he may strengthen you with power through his Spirit in your inner being, so that Christ may dwell in your hearts through faith. And I pray that you, being rooted and established in love, may have power, together with all the Lord's holy people, to grasp how wide and long and high and deep is the love of Christ, and to know love that surpasses knowledge-that you may be filled to the measure of all the fullness of God." (Ephesians 3:16-19 NIV)

My mom has several china sets. They are all different in sizes and designs. They come from different places in the world. They are very beautiful pieces of art.

She has them displayed in a china cabinet, so all who come in can view and admire them. Whenever someone asks about them, she tells the story of how and where she got them.

She also has another set that she bought from a garage sale that she displays in another china cabinet.

Around the holiday season, my mom sets the table. It's funny how she always uses the set that she bought from the garage sale. So, when company comes, they can view a beautiful table setting and use the china when eating or drinking.

I also noticed although she has had different sets of china and dishes throughout the year; this set has been around the longest. It seems to me to be the special china set. She uses it all the time, while the other sets haven't been used at all.

The other sets just sit there in the china cabinet looking pretty, just sitting there for people to look at and admire. But they are never used.

One day while sitting admiring the different china sets, my mind began to wander (as it always does). I began to compare the people that come to church with the china sets.

There are those that come to every service and sit on the pews time after time. Some never get involved in any of God's work. They are like the china sets that sit in the china cabinet year after year, all dressed up looking pretty—never appearing to have any desire to be used and never making themselves available to be used by God. Never asking to be filled with His spirit or never attend teaching services to be filled with His word. Therefore, can never be used as a witness for Him. They just come Sunday after Sunday sitting in the pews all dressed up looking pretty but never fellowship with God or other believers.

But then there are those who have a desire to be used by God. (Luke 10:2) reads, Therefore said he unto them, the harvest truly is great, but the laborers are few: pray ye, therefore, the Lord of the harvest, that he would send forth laborers into his harvest. This text lets us know that there is work to be done. That we as believers are not just to enter God's kingdom to sit and do nothing. We are to enter into His kingdom, ready to be filled with His spirit *(Ephesians 3:16-19)*. We are to desire to be filled that we may minister to others. We should make ourselves available to be used by God that others may know Him. We should always fellowship with God and His people to be equipped to minister to the hungry and thirsty, whether it is spiritual or physical.

Yes, I would definitely want to be like the special china set. So that when God calls the thirsty and hungry to His supper table, they can eat and drink from me and be filled.

A Word of Wisdom

The harvest is truly plenteous, but the laborers are few.

We must be about what the Master has called us to do.

So, when the table is set, and His guest have sat down,

would you be a part of His special china set, so the thirsty and

hungry can eat and drink from you like you are eating and

drinking from me now.

The Love Relationship

"Dear friends, let us love one another, for love comes from God. Everyone who loves has been born of God and knows God. Whoever does not love does not know God, because God is love."
(1John 4: 7-8 NIV)

"This is love: not that we loved God, but that he loved us and sent his Son as an atoning sacrifice for our sins." (1John 4:10 NIV)

"For God so loved the world that he gave his one and only Son, that whoever believes in him shall not perish but have eternal life." (John 3:16 NIV)

The meaning of a lot of things has been wrongly defined in the world today, whether by word, action or deed. For example, the words love relationship. These words have been tossed around like a hot potato, especially in relationships.

One may tell their companion they love them, marry them and a few months, years and sometimes a few days later tell them they want a divorce. Then off they go looking for another someone to love, and the cycle goes on. They continue this cycle, not realizing that it's not love at all, but lust. They continue to search for that love that is so desired by all (being that everyone needs love) they never find it.

As I wrestled with this thought over and over in my mind, I began to focus on different relationships. I would see and hear of different couples that appeared to be madly in love. Then a little while later, I would see and hear of the relationships ending. The more I pondered this love thing over and over again, I found myself asking of God.

Why is it that people call everything love that isn't love and cannot recognize love when they have it? And He answered, "How can one recognize love when they have never had a relationship with love, for God is Love."

Although the question of love had appeared so complex when looking to natural relationships for an answer. It became so elementary and so clear when I asked God about it.

The Bible tells us that God is love *(1John 4: 7-8)*. He loves us with unconditional love *(1John 4:10)*. He doesn't love us for a time and then (for whatever reason some may have) kick us in a corner like an old pair of shoes. Then go out looking for a new pair. He loves us with an everlasting love. He loves us with Agape love, a quality of love, *(John 15:13)*. He loves us with a love that will never end.

There is no better teacher on the subject of the love relationship than God Himself.

So, if you are looking for true love and want to know when you have truly found it, you must know *Love (John 3:16)*. You must accept Him into your heart and get to know Him. Then and only then can you have a true love relationship with another (The book of Song of Solomon).

A Word of Wisdom

As I walked along in this old world,

I was living my life as a foolish young girl.

Looking for love in all the wrong places,

searching for love in all the wrong faces.

Relationships here, relationships there,

couldn't find the right one anywhere.

Then I heard a voice talking to me,

He said, "I'm the one you're looking for, I'm love you see."

I asked, "How can I know that this love is true."

He said, "I loved you so much that I died for you."

I said, "How can you live, if for me your life you gave."

He said, "Nothing could stop me not even the grave."

I finally found true love in this world,

And I no longer live as a foolish young girl.

We've established a relationship,

And He has proved His love is true.

So, if you're looking for love,

He tells me to tell you,

He loves and died for you.

The Faucet

*"That he lavished on us. With all wisdom and understanding, he
made known to us the mystery of his will according to his good
pleasure, which he purposed in Christ" (Ephesians1:8-9 NIV)*

"Do not quench the Spirit." (1 Thessalonians 5:19 NIV)

*"Therefore, my dear friends, as you have always obeyed-not
only in my presence, but now much more in my absence-
continue to work out your salvation with fear and trembling, for
it is God who works in you to will and to act in order to fulfill his
good purpose." (Philippians 2:12-13 NIV)*

*'God also testified to it by signs, wonders and various miracles,
and by gifts of the Holy Spirit distributed according to his will."
(Hebrews 2:4 NIV)*

We were having a women's retreat. We were to be shut
in and up all night to be in the presence of the Lord.
We were to pray, discuss and meditate on His word.
Also, each woman was to share about their personal relationship
with the Lord. While having our discussion, one of the women
(the one in charge and had organized the retreat) asked what we
thought our specific gift or purpose was.

And as each individual gave their answer, I noticed there was a sense
of satisfaction and pride between that individual and the one who

had asked the question. It was as if the individual answering was answering in a way only to please the one who had asked.

But as I waited for my turn to answer, I couldn't think of any specific gift. I had never thought of it in that manner. I just wanted to be used, however, and whenever God wanted to use me *(Ephesians1:8-9)*. I didn't want to limit Him *(1 Thessalonians 5:19)*.

So, my turn came up, and I answered, "I'm open for God to use me however He pleases." Not pleased with my answer, the one in charge of the retreat responded, "That's fine and good, but there is a specific thing that God has gifted you to do."

Not knowing how to explain to the group what I believed and had experienced in my relationship with the Lord, I began asking of Him.

While the one in charge tried to explain and convince me to give a satisfactory answer, I secretly asked the Holy Spirit to help me to get it over to them what I believed.

The discussion went on between the other women and me. In a forceful kind of way, they were trying to convince me to believe the way they did. I did not believe that way and did not want to *(Philippians 2:12-13)*. And not to my surprise, I got an answer.

I was instructed to go to the kitchen faucet. With me believing He could use me and anything else anyway He wanted, I obeyed His instruction.

So I asked all the women to go to the kitchen sink with me. I began to explain to them that we are like channels or vessels that God uses to work or flow through *(Hebrews 2:4)*. I turned the faucet on slightly, and the water began to drip, one drop at a time.

I explained to the women that some of God's people limit Him in using them in that manner. For example, one may have a great singing voice. So they only allow God to use them in ministry through song. I turned the faucet on a little more, so the water flowed a little more. I continued to explain how others will allow God to use them a little more as long as it was comfortable and gave them self-satisfaction (something they liked doing). Then I turned the faucet all the way on, so the water flowed fully and freely. I began to explain to the women that there are those who are fully open for God to use them in any way He pleases. I told them that I believe God uses me in all sorts of ways. Whether it was being the speaker to a congregation (the one delivering a message to the church), or cleaning the church building, He could use me for mission work, caring for the sick. He has used me to fix a car for the poor and even give a car to the poor. He has used me in the ministry of song and directing a choir, and the list goes on.

I want to be the kind of channel that God can flow freely through. I told them I didn't want to and will not limit God in what He could or wanted to do through me. I was His and was created for His good pleasure. In other words, I was created for Him to use however He desires to.

A Word of Wisdom

God gives us gifts, makes us vessels, and channels whatever he

chooses. Let us always be mindful that we are created for His

use. So, don't limit Him. Like a fully opened faucet,

let Him freely flow through you.

Allowing Him to do whatever He desires to do.

Fill My Cups

"*Whoever believes in me, as Scripture has said, rivers of living water will flow from within them." (John 7:38 NIV)*

"*When they had finished eating, Jesus said to Simon Peter, 'Simon son of John, do you love me more than these?" "Yes, Lord," he said, "you know that I love you." Jesus said, "Feed my lambs." Again Jesus said, "Simon son of John, do you love me?" He answered, 'Yes, Lord you know that I love you," Jesus said, 'Take care of my sheep." (John 21:15-16 NIV)*

It's five o'clock in the morning. I'm headed to the garage to fellowship with the Lord. I made my usual stop at the coffee pot for a cup of coffee.

This was a daily routine for me. It was also the best part of my day.

I knew the Lord would be waiting there for me. We had an appointment seven days a week no matter what.

I would get up and go to the coffee pot to make coffee and get a cup of coffee. Then go into the garage where I had placed a table and chair to spend two hours or so with the Lord.

Why the garage? Well, there was no television and no other interruptions, just the Lord and me sitting in His presence.

Sometimes it would be hard for me to sleep at night, anticipating getting up the next morning to spend time with Lord. I knew without a shadow of a doubt that He would impart wisdom to me. He would fill me a little more each day. I would sit at His feet like an empty vessel before a full fountain waiting to be filled.

Whether it was winter, summer, spring or fall, we would meet in the garage. This had gone on for years.

So, this particular morning, as I picked up the pitcher to pour coffee into the cup, I heard, "Fill my cups with what I have filled you with." It stunned me! I was frightened at first. I realized it was a call, a commission, a command! I almost dropped the pitcher!

He was showing me that He had taken me to a higher level of service. I was to become like the pitcher. The way I had sat before the fountain as an empty vessel waiting to be filled, I was now a fountain full of living water *(John 7:38)*. The Lord was filling me that whenever there was an empty vessel sat before me, they could be filled.

You see, all that He had given me, I was not to keep for myself only. I was to share it. I was to give it away. I was to make other disciples for Him, like His son Jesus did.

Although at the time, I didn't know how I would be able to carry out this great task, I said yes, Lord.

Beloved, if we would sit before the Lord (That fountain of living water), we will continually be filled. And our vessel will overflow. And whatever He imparts in us, we should share with others. For what would it profit Him if we kept it all just for ourselves *(John 21:15-16)*.

A Word of Wisdom

Lord make us vessels of living water.

Fill us up that we may share with others.

Sitting at Your feet day by day, being filled with Your good news, not just for us Lord, but that we may become a vessel, a river of living water for You.

The Bride

"Before a young woman's turn came to go into King Zerxes, she had to complete twelve months of beauty treatments prescribed for the women, six months with oil of myrrh and six with perfumes and cosmetics." (Esther 2:12 NIV)

"As a young man marries a young woman, so will your Builder marry you; as a bridegroom rejoices over his bride, so will your God rejoice over you." (Isaiah 62:5 NIV)

"And to present her to himself as a radiant church, without stain or wrinkle or any other blemish, but holy and blameless."
(Ephesians 5:27 NIV)

Weddings are one of the most beautiful occasions a person can attend. It's a joyous event. It's a time when family and friends come together, feast together and fellowship together. And two people are united together in holy matrimony, becoming one.

I have attended many weddings. I have experienced different cultural ceremonies passed down from generation to generation. Although there is a traditional wedding, there are some families that have started their own tradition. But no matter what kind of wedding is planned, there must be a relationship before the occasion.

People marry at all ages, being that you're never too old to marry when you find true love. Although this is true, I want to focus on the traditional way leading to a marriage. The kind most people dream of experiencing and hope their children will experience. You know when two people meet and go on a date. They become fond of each other. They schedule more dates, and the courtship begins. And sometime during the courtship, they fall in love. A good relationship develops and then comes the engagement. They make a commitment to one another.

They promise to never be with another. Although they have not yet reached the point of the marriage ceremony, they already, in a sense, belong to one another.

Then the day draws near for them to be joined together. The time that they so eagerly and patiently waited for. The day that they have been preparing for.

And traditionally, the bride goes through more preparation than the groom because the groom is usually already prepared.

You know like Esther *(Esther 2:12)*. She went through a period of preparation and purification so that she would be at her best because she was chosen to marry the king.

She was also a virgin, which from the beginning, is how it was ordained of God to be.

And then the day of the wedding arrives. And the ceremony begins.

Awe! And there she stands. Beautiful! Vibrant! Arrayed as she has never been before. Young, untouched by any other. Pure, having been set aside for the one who chose her, the one who loves her.

Yes, a young virgin. Traditionally so young that she appears flawless. Her skin having no age spots, wrinkles or blemishes.

She is to be joined to the one that she loves more than any other. And at the time of marriage, there is nothing more important to the bride than how she appears to her groom. She does not want the groom to see any flaws. Nothing can be out of place. It's so important to her to please him. She wants to look her best for him.

Dressed in her white gown, representing her purification. Yes, and at that moment, I am sure that she appears to her groom as being flawless!

I guess I appreciate the traditional way of courtship, engagement, and marriage because it's the best illustration of Christ and His Church *(Isaiah 62:5)*.

Yes, it's very similar to when I met Him. We began to spend time together. And the more time we spent together, I realized that He loved me like no other. And this caused me to fall in love with Him. Knowing that He was committed to me, I also committed my life to Him. I began to spend more time with Him, more than I did with any other. We were getting to know each other. We belong to one another. We are preparing for that joyous occasion when we will become one.

And knowing that my groom is already prepared, I must get prepared for that great day. I want to be my best. No matter what age I am. Spiritually speaking, I want to be like that traditional bride. I want to be purified. I want to be dressed in purity without spots or wrinkles. No blemishes, appearing not to have been touched by the world. I want to be a picture of beauty to my groom.

(*Ephesians 5:27*) speaks of how we will be prepared for our Groom (Jesus Christ). We will be without spot, wrinkle or blemish. We are set aside, being cleansed, and purified with the washing of the water, by the word of God. We will be presented to Him as a glorious bride.

A Word of Wisdom

Let us make preparation before it's too late,

while we anticipate that most important date.

We being as a bride, and the Lord being as our groom,

we must get ready for he is coming soon.

So let him wash you, purify you, taking your imperfections

away, that we may be presented a glorious church on that day.

The Light

"Long life is in her right hand; in her left hand are riches and honor." (Proverbs 3:16 NIV)

"Your word is a lamp for my feet, a light on my path." (Psalms 119:105 NIV)

"Dear friends, do not believe every spirit, but test the spirits to see whether they are from God, because many false prophets have gone out into the world. This is how you can recognize the Spirit of God: Every spirit that acknowledges that Jesus Christ has come in the flesh is from God, but every spirit that does not acknowledge Jesus is not from God, This is the spirit of the antichrist, which you have heard is coming and even now is already in the world. You, dear children, are from God and have overcome them, because the one who is in you is greater than the one who is in the world. They are from the world. You dear children, are from God and have overcome them, because the one who is in you is greater than the one who is in the world. They are from the world and therefore speak from the viewpoint of the world, and the world listens to them. We are from God, and whoever knows God listens to us; but whoever is not from God does not listen to us. This is how we recognize the Spirit of truth and the spirit of falsehood. Dear friends, let us love one another, for love comes from God. Everyone who loves has been born of God and knows God. Whoever does not love does not

know God, because God is love. This is how God showed his love
among us: He sent his one and only Son as an atoning sacrifice
for our sins. Dear friends, since God so loved us, we also ought to
love one another. No one has ever seen God; but if we love one
another, God lives in us and his love is made complete in us. This
is how we know that we live in him and he in us: He has given us
his Spirit. And we have seen and testify that the Father has sent
his Son to be the Savior of the world." (John1:1-14 NIV)

"You guide me with your counsel, and afterward you will take
me into glory." (Psalms 73:24 NIV)

Driving in thick fog can be very hazardous, especially at night. If it wasn't for the streetlights and the lights on the building, it would be impossible to stay on course. Reflective street signs are also beneficial when driving in fog at night. When the car lights reflect off the signs, it helps us know where we are and that we are going in the right direction.

In the fall and winter months, I traveled in the fog a lot. My daughter and I lived in a small town a few miles from the rest of my family.

We would drive from our home to my mother's and other family member's homes every now and then to visit for the day. Our plan would be to get back home before nightfall. But sometimes we would be enjoying the visit so much until we would lose track of time.

One day we headed home right about dusk. The sun had just about gone all the way down, and the fog had begun to roll in. By the time we made it to the highway, we were in a thick blanket of fog. The visibility was at a minimum. And nightfall had come.

As we drove up the highway and came to the edge of town, the visibility was even less. I drove up the highway slowly, using the street signs and lights on the buildings as a guide to staying on course.

The highway was a four-lane highway. There were two lanes for west-bound traffic, and two for east-bound traffic. There was a median in the middle of the highway separating the east and west-bound lanes.

I continued to focus on the lights in the almost black dark night. I drove on the outside lane because with the fog being so thick, I didn't want to have to change lanes if a car needed to pass.

Suddenly, I saw two lights that appeared to be coming towards me on the same side of the highway. As I drove along, the lights came closer, and I realized it was a car. Someone was driving on the wrong side of the highway on the inside lane. "What are they doing?" I said. "They are driving on the wrong side of the highway!" I said. I eased on by the car and continued my journey home.

While wondering how that could happen, I began to pray that the driver would realize they were driving on the wrong side of the highway before it was too late. I also prayed that they would make it to their destiny safe.

As I began to focus on the lights again, I searched for the store lights that sat on the left side of the highway at the edge of the town that we lived in.

Further down, there was another store on the right side of the highway on the corner of the street we lived on.

I knew they would be lit up. This would help me to know I had almost made it home and be able to make the turn onto the street we live on. And keeping a focus on the lights, I did just that.

After making the right turn, I began searching for the yellow light knowing that would be home. Because of the fog, I would always leave my yellow porch light on to easily identify my home if we arrived after dark. Finally, we made it home safe.

As I lay in bed that night, I wondered about the driver that drove on the wrong side of the highway. I wondered if they made it to their destination safely. I thought if they had just kept their focus on the lights and signs as their guide. I also thought, did they even know where they were going or had they lost their way?

Reflecting on the situation, I began to think about our Christian journey. When we can't see our way clearly. When we are going through trials and tribulation and life seems to be so dark. Sometimes in those times, we feel we have lost our way. Most times, when going through tough times, the enemy will try and convince us that we are not on the right path. And sometimes he gets us off the right path if we don't stay focused on the light of the word. There are times when we don't know which way to go in life *(Proverbs 3:16)*. Our sight becomes dim. We can't see clear enough to make the right decisions or what steps to take when going through trials, even when we are not sure where we stand with God. We can always look to His word and find out if we are with Him or not *(Psalms 119:105)*. Even when we are lost in a dark and evil world and looking for a way out, the word tells us Jesus is the way *(John1:1-14)*.

Life can become overwhelming and different circumstances can dim our view. But if we just stay focused on the light, God's word and allow the Holy Spirit to be our guide, We will make it to our destiny heaven, our home, safe *(Psalms 73:24)*.

A Word of Wisdom

As we are on our journey, going to and from each day,

stay focused on the light, that He may lead the way.

The good times clear as day, the hard times dark as night.

The unsure times are like traveling through fog,

But just stay focused on the light.

And if you ever feel you lost your way, and all hope seems to be

gone, look to the light, He will carefully guide you on.

Stay focused on the light and never just roam,

that when the journeys over, the light will guide you safely home.

A New Life

"Therefore, since we are surrounded by such a great cloud of witnesses, let us throw off everything that hinders and the sin that so easily entangles. And let us run with perseverance the race marked out for us." (Hebrews 12:1 NIV)

"Brothers and sisters, I do not consider myself yet to have taken hold of it. But one thing I do: Forgetting what is behind and straining toward what is ahead, I press on toward the goal to win the prize for which God has called me heavenward in Christ Jesus." (Philippians 3:13-14 NIV)

"The thief comes only to steal and kill and destroy; I have come that they may have life, and have it to the full." (John 10:10 NIV)

I had been through a divorce. Most people that have experienced a divorce know some of the effects it can have on you. It's not easy. And if you were married for a long period of time, you accumulate a lot of stuff. Whether it's materialistic or emotional, we can accumulate all kinds of memorabilia.

Although we are sure the relationship or marriage is over, we tend to store away things pertaining to it.

Even in our heart and mind, we store away a lot of memories and emotions. Hearing a certain song will send us strolling back down memory lane.

Several years had passed since the divorce. I had moved on with my life and had met a very nice gentleman. We met at my job.

I was a service station attendant, and he was from another state. His job had brought him to the town where I lived. He would stop to get gas at the station where I worked. We dated for a while, fell in love, and got engaged. We were to be married a few months later.

We began making plans where we would live after we were married. He was from Illinois, and I lived in a small town in New Mexico. Most of my family was also in New Mexico, and he was on the road a lot with his job. So, for the time being, we chose New Mexico, knowing that I wasn't used to living in a big city. He also didn't like the idea of me being in Illinois alone while he was away from home.

The decision was made. We were to live in the house that I was currently living in for the time being.

I needed to prepare for my new husband. I knew I had to get rid of some things in the house to make room for his things. So I began to go through the rooms of the house, closets, drawers and all the other places we tend to store things away.

While doing so, I noticed how much stuff I still had from the first marriage. I found cards, pictures, keepsakes, even some of my ex-husband's things he had stored away and forgotten about. Although that part of my life was over (and I knew it was), I still had so much of it still in my house. It was surprising to me. Even if it was packed up and stored away, it should have been gone, done away with. I didn't need it anymore and didn't want it. It was just taking up space.

I didn't want to go back down memory lane. I wanted to move forward. That life was over, and I had long started a new life. I had even moved from my hometown to another town and back to my hometown again. I had been carrying all that extra baggage around with me all those years.

I thought to myself, this is crazy! I must get rid of it all! And I really didn't want my new husband to come across any of it after he moved in. How uncomfortable it would make him feel to find things in our home from my past life with my ex as if I were holding on to it in some sneaky way.

With that thought in mind, I began searching diligently for anything that had anything to do with that past life. I didn't want any part of it left in the house. I had no room for anything from the old life.

I wanted my husband to feel welcome. I wanted him to know that this was his home. I wanted to set the house up so my husband would comfortably dwell there. I wanted it to be a place where we could start and build our new life together.

While going through the house trying to accomplish my goal, I began thinking about how we as believers carry extra baggage around from our old life. I thought we have it all packed up and stored away. Then every now and then, we go strolling back down memory lane *(Hebrews 12:1)*. We sometimes carry so much from our past life like, hate, bitterness, gossip, envy, jealousy, lust, hurts, all kinds of spirits and old ways; until we haven't made room enough for the Spirit of God into our lives and abide.

We should search our hearts and lives daily, making sure there is nothing in us that would grieve the Holy Spirit and keep him from feeling welcome. Our hearts need to become a place where the spirit of God can abide while we live our new life together *(Philippians 3:13-14)*. This way, we may experience our new life more abundantly *(John 10:10)*.

A Word of Wisdom

When my old life has passed away,

Lord remind me to do spiritual inventory day by day,

to see if there be

any enemies from the past still in me.

Then help me to do what I need to do,

that You may live in me.

And that I may begin my new life with you.

Babes

"I am going to send you what my Father has promised; but stay in the city until you have been clothed with power from on high."
(Luke 24:49 NIV)

"Go! I am sending you out like lambs among wolves."
(Luke 10:3 NIV)

"I know that after I leave, savage wolves will come in among you and will not spare the flock," (Acts 20:29 NIV)

Newborn babies are very vulnerable when they arrive in this world. They become exposed to a whole new way of living. Basically, all they can do to survive is eat, when fed, sleep and pass toxins from their tiny, fragile bodies. Everything else they need is left up to the one or ones who care for them. They totally depend on the one they have been given to.

Still unable to do much for themselves, most babies can sit up on their own by the age of four months. Then they learn to crawl, being able to move about on their own. By now, they are able to feed themselves what we call finger foods. Also, during the crawling stage, they learn to pull themselves up and stand, holding on to whatever they pull themselves up on. There is a lot of other things they learn at this stage in life.

Then comes walking. By now, they have become much more independent. Yet and still cannot do much for themselves to survive.

There was a time when babies spent at least the first four years of their lives in the home, bonding, and learning from their parents and other siblings. They would not be in too many different environments. They were kept in a controlled environment. In an environment where everyone was pretty much alike and lived by the same principles.

At birth, they were held close to their mother's bosom, being fed repeatedly. Being nurtured, trained and equipped to a certain degree, preparing to go outside of that controlled environment. And by the time they were old enough to attend school, they were no longer babes. They can do much, much more for themselves. And they have a better sense of what's right and wrong.

They are now able to go out, still needing the constant supervision of an adult or a much older sibling and inter-mingling with all sorts of people. And usually they are under a different supervision other than their parents. And they are amongst different children other than their siblings, coming from all kinds of households. They are cast into an environment of multiple characters, beliefs, cultures, habits and much more that they can be influenced by.

With my babies, it was very important for me that they stay in that controlled environment for the first four years of their lives. It gave me a chance to impart in them what they needed most to sustain them to go out and face the world. This is crucial! Not only as natural babies but also as babes in Christ.

And as a babe in Christ, it helped me to understand when Jesus said in *(Luke 24:49)* "...tarry ye in Jerusalem until ye be endued with power from on high." He knew what was ahead. He knew with his disciples going out into the world, they would need power from a higher authority to sustain them. He would no longer be with them in the flesh to walk and talk with them. But they would be sustained.

He had imparted in them His teachings. He had trained them. They had been in a somewhat controlled environment, in preparation to go out like lambs amongst wolves *(Luke10:3)*.

The Lord's disciples needed the Holy Spirit to comfort them. Also, to lead and guide them, keeping them in the way they should go, and continually reminding them in a spirit of what had been imparted in them *(Acts 20:29)*.

So many times, I see babes in Christ go out and be devoured by different predators lying wait for them out in the world because they ignore what Jesus said. They don't stay in a controlled environment under supervision in order to be equipped enough to face the world. They don't allow themselves to be nurtured, taught and trained.

It is so important for babes in Christ to tarry in God's house amongst other brothers and sisters in Christ. And it's more important to stay under the supervision of a good leader—one who helps you grow in wisdom and knowledge. And most of all, tarry, waiting to receive power from on high. Then when the time comes for one to go out into the world, yet still needing the supervision of a higher authority, they will be prepared and equipped to go.

A Word of Wisdom

As newborn babes in Christ,

there is very little that we can do,

and very little that we know.

So, it is very important,

to stay in a safe controlled environment,

being trained, taught and nurtured while we grow.

Waiting to be endued with a power from on high,

a sustaining power sent to us here below,

so when the time comes we will know.

We are prepared, equipped, and sure of the way we should go.

The Water

"When a Samaritan woman came to draw water, Jesus said to her, 'Will you give me a drink?' (His disciples had gone into the town to buy food.) The Samaritan woman said to him, 'You are a Jew and I am a Samaritan woman. How can you ask me for a drink?' (For Jews do not associate with Samaritans.) Jesus answered her, 'If you knew the gift of God and who it is that asks you for a drink, you would have asked him and he would have given you living water.' 'Sir,' the woman said, 'you have nothing to draw with and the well is deep. Where can you get this living water? Are you greater than our Father Jacob, who gave us the well and drank from it himself, as did also his sons and his livestock?' Jesus answered, 'Everyone who drinks this water will be thirsty again, but whoever drinks the water I give them will never thirst. Indeed, the water I give them will become in them a spring of water welling up to eternal life.' (John 4:7-14 NIV)

"The woman said to him, 'Sir, give me this water so that I won't get thirsty and have to keep coming here to draw water." He told her, 'Go, call your husband and come back." 'I have no husband,' she replied. Jesus said to her, 'You are right when you say you have no husband. The fact is, you have had five husbands, and the man you now have is not your husband. What you have just said is quite true." 'Sir,' the woman said, 'I can see that you are a prophet. Our ancestors on this mountain, but you Jews claim that

*the place where we must worship is in Jerusalem." 'Woman,"
Jesus replied, 'believe me, a time is coming when you will worship
the Father neither on this mountain nor in Jerusalem. You
Samaritans worship what you do not know; we worship what we
do know, for salvation is from the Jews. Yet a time is coming and
has now come when the true worshipers will worship the Father
in the Spirit and in truth, for they are the kind of worshipers the
Father seeks. God is spirit, and his worshipers must worship in the
Spirit and in truth." The woman said, 'I know that Messiah' (called
Christ) 'is coming. When he comes, he will explain everything to
us." Then Jesus declared, 'I, the one speaking to you-I am he.' Just
then his disciples returned and were surprised to find him talking
with a woman. But no one asked, 'What do you want' or 'Why are
you talking with her?' Then, leaving her water jar, the woman
went back to the town and said to the people, 'Come, see a man
who told me everything I ever did. Could this be the Messiah?'
They came out of the town and made their way toward him."*
(John 4: 15-30 NIV)

Every year around springtime, I would start paying attention to
the grass. Not only in my yard but also in other yards as I
passed by. I would watch it (the grass) turn from a pale yellow
to having a light green hue, although the spring showers had not yet
begun. Seeing this, I would begin to water my grass. I would water in the
morning and evening, anticipating for the grass to become darker and
richer in color.

After watering my lawn every day for a period of time, I would
realize that it was just not enough. The grass was not turning

green fast enough. While some areas of the yard were darker, other areas were still yellow with a light green hue.

Frustrated from not getting the results I wanted as quickly as I wanted, I began to wonder if I was wasting my time. I would even come to the point of feeling like giving up. But still, I kept watering.

But right before I would give up, in would come the spring showers. The first one was not very heavy or very long. But it was enough for me not to have to water the day it rained.

As I prepared to water the afternoon of the second day, I noticed the color of the grass was now greener with a light green hue. There was no yellow hue at all.

Wow! I thought what a little shower from heaven could do! All the watering I had done didn't do half as much as one shower from heaven.

While watering the yard, I kept thinking about how the rainwater made such a big difference when applied to the grass than the water from the faucet. The rainwater had not been tampered with. It had come straight from heaven. And the water from the faucet had been through a process. It's was not in its original state. It had been tampered with by the hands of man. The faucet was not as effective as the rainwater. Evidently, when man tampered with the water, it changed the quality of the water.

This changed my perspective on watering. So I began praying for more rain, knowing that I would get better results.

As I prayed, while still watering the grass, a revelation began to unfold. I began to see how important it is to be in the presence of the Lord when no one else is around. Sitting in His presence, receiving the word straight from Him *(1 Kings 10:38-42)*.

Spiritually speaking, we may go to different services listening to different preachers, teachers and so on, drinking water that is supplied through mankind. And in a lot of cases, it doesn't have the full effect.

But sitting at the feet of Jesus, enquiring of Him, and learning from Him makes such a big difference. Drinking from a fountain of living water. Pure water, not having been touched by man. Water coming straight from the master himself.

He is that living water *(John 4:7-14)*. A well of water with a quality that is sure to affect the growth of a thirsty believer.

Although we have other wells that have been provided for us to drink from when thirsty, we must never forget that Jesus is the most important and effective one. We must take time to sit under that fountain of water flowing full and free to all who will take time to receive. He is that living water *(John 4: 15-30)*.

A Word of Wisdom

Like the grass in spring, we too need water to grow.

Though some receive water day by day,

Very little growth in their lives do they show.

Like the grass being watered by man

Does not provide all that I need

We need to be watered with the living water

In order to succeed.

So if you desire growth at a different degree,

You must make fellowship with Jesus Christ become priority

Receiving water of the best quality.

For he is the living water, provided through love

And he desires to do to us, what the water does to the grass,

When showers down from up above.

The Markings and the Piercings Guidelines

'Do not cut your bodies for the dead or put tattoo marks on yourselves. I am the Lord." (Leviticus 19:28 NIV)

"Therefore, I urge you, brothers and sisters, in view of God's mercy, to offer your bodies as a living sacrifice, holy and pleasing to God-this is your true and proper worship. Do not conform to the pattern of this world, but be transformed by the renewing of your mind. Then you will be able to test and approve what God's will is – his good, pleasing and perfect will." (Romans 12:1-2 NIV)

"Therefore, since we are surrounded by such a great cloud of witnesses, let us throw off everything that hinders and the sin that so easily entangles. And let us run with perseverance the race marked out for us," (Hebrews 4:12 NIV)

"Leave them; they are blind guides. If the blind lead the blind, both will fall into a pit." (Matthew 15:14 NIV)

'You show that you are a letter from Christ, the result of our ministry, written not with ink but with the Spirit of the living God, not on tablets of stone but on tablets of human hearts." (2 Corinthians 3:3 NIV)

"They will see his face, and his name will be on their foreheads."
(Revelation 22:4 NIV)

It's funny how people will allow different things, action and other people to influence them.

Whether it's clothing, lifestyles, fads, or trends.

Down through the years, different trends develop and then fade away, making way for a new one. Different movements come and go. Language has even had its part in it, while people slung around slang words. Yes, whatever was cool and happening.

This particular period of time, it seemed that almost everyone around me were getting tattoos or piercings from the young to the almost old. Every time I turned around, someone else had gotten a tattoo or something pierced on their body. I seemed as if it had become an epidemic. I would see anything from eyebrows to belly buttons being pierced. And heard of some other things being pierced, that I can't even imagine or mention. And not to mention the tattoos. Some of them were so large that I knew they took hours to do.

I know getting a piercing or tattoo is painful. I would ask sometime when someone was showing theirs off, "Did that hurt?" They would reply, "No, it didn't hurt." I would think to myself, sure it didn't, while knowing the process it took to get a piercing or a tattoo. But yet and still, I would see more and more people getting them.

With me being a Christian, I could see how people that were not would fall into a fad like that. But when I saw the volume of people professing to be Christians getting them, I was shocked *(Lev.19:28)*! There was a lot! And they were of all ages. And if they hadn't already gotten one or the other or both, they were anticipating it. And the only reason some of them had was because they were too young or didn't have the money to yet. It had become so bad until the expression, "There's too many leaders and not enough followers," appeared to be an untruth.

In this case, it seemed to be no leaders, but all followers (one of another). And if it were a leader of leaders, who was it (concerning those who attended church regularly). And those that were followers, who or what were they following *(Romans 12:1-2)*.

Upon receiving their first tattoo or piercing, they were allowing someone that they didn't really even know to pierce or mark their body. They were trusting in someone they really didn't even know. The only knowledge they really had of them was what they had probably been told. And they were trusting in the word of the one that had told them. Seeing how they were so eager to allow someone that they really knew nothing about inflicting pain on them and receive something that didn't really even matter was puzzling. And it was even more puzzling that they were willing to go through the pain for something that was basically worthless.

As I sat one day trying to process and make sense of it all, I heard, "They won't let me pierce *(Heb. 4:12)* and write my word upon the table of their hearts." It was amazing!

When I heard that which was spoken. I had a sorrowful feeling. It's sad how people reject the Lord over and over after hearing his word over and over, how they follow after everybody and everything allowing it or them to influence their lives *(Matt 15:14)*. It's sad how people will mimic any and everything (become copycats) just trying to fit in, trying to belong. People will take the risk of pain and whatever else that comes along with piercings and tattoos (markings) they will trust in the words of man when told who the best is to go to, receiving them. While in all their getting, the Lord is crying out let me pierce and write my words upon the tablet of your heart *(2 Cor. 3:3)* and write His name upon their foreheads *(Rev. 22:4)*.

A Word of Wisdom

There are so many things that can influence us in the world

today. All kinds of spirits trying to conform us in every way.

Giving way to them in ignorance, in some we take part.

Receiving unto ourselves their piercing and marks.

This may be stepping on some toes (as the old saying goes)

But I'm more concerned about saving of souls.

The bible tells us not to be like the world, from it we are to be set

apart, And if you don't know how to be, I'll give you a start.

Hear, believe, repent, and accept Jesus

And let Him write His word upon and pierce your heart.

The Manifestation

"But seek first his kingdom and his righteousness, and all these things will be given to you as well." (Matthew 6:33 NIV)

"If any of you lacks wisdom, you should as God, who gives generously to all without finding fault, and it will be given to you." (James 1:5 NIV)

"He was despised and rejected by mankind, a man of suffering, and familiar with pain. Like one from whom people hide their faces he was despised, and we held him in low esteem. Surely he took up our pain and bore our suffering, yet we considered him punished by God, stricken by him, and afflicted. But he was pierced for our transgressions, he was crushed for our iniquities: the punishment that brought us peace was on him, and by his wounds we are healed. We all, like sheep, have gone astray, each of us has turned to our own way; and the Lord has laid on him the iniquity of us all. He was oppressed and afflicted, yet he did not open his mouth, he was led like a lamb to the slaughter, and as a sheep before its shearers is silent, so he did not open his mouth. By oppression and judgement he was taken away. Yet who of his generation protested? For he was cut off from the land of the living; for the transgression of my people he was punished. He was assigned a grave with the wicked, and with the rich in his death, though he had done no violence, nor was any deceit in his mouth. Yet it was the Lord's will to crush him and cause him to

suffer for sin, he will see his offspring and prolong his days, and the will of the Lord will prosper in his hand. After he has suffered, he will see the light of life and be satisfied; by his knowledge my righteous servant will justify many, and he will bear their iniquities. Therefore I will give him a portion among the great, and he will divide the spoils with the strong, because he poured out his life unto death, and was numbered with the transgressors. For he bore the sin of many, and made intercession for the transgressors. (Isaiah 53:3-12 NIV)

"Be alert and of sober mind. Your enemy the devil prowls around like a roaring lion looking for someone to devour."
(1 Peter 5:8 NIV)

"For God so loved the world that he gave his one and only Son, that whoever believes in him shall not perish but have eternal life." (John 3:16 NIV)

"A large number of people followed him, including women who mourned and wailed for him. Jesus turned and said to them, 'Daughters of Jerusalem, do not weep for me; weep for yourselves and for your children. For the time will come when you will say, 'Blessed are the childless women, the wombs that never bore and the breasts that never nursed!' Then "they will say to the mountains, 'Fall on us!" and to the hills, "Cover us!" For if people do these things when the tree is green, what will happen when it is dry?" Two other men, both criminals, were also led out with him to be executed. When they came to the place called the Skull, they crucified him there, along with the criminals-one on his right, the other on his left. Jesus said

"Father, forgive them, for they do not know what they are doing." And they divided up his clothes by casting lots. The people stood watching, and the rulers even sneered at him. They said, "He saved others; let him save himself if he is God's Messiah, the Chosen One." The soldiers also came up and mocked him. They offered him wine vinegar and said "If you are the king of the Jews, save yourself." There was a written notice above him, which read:

THIS IS THE KING OF THE JEWS.

One of the criminals who hung there hurled insults at him: "Aren't you the Messiah? Save yourself and us!" But the other criminal rebuked him. "Don't you fear God," he said, "since you are under the same sentence? We are punished justly, for we are getting what our deeds deserve. But this man has done nothing wrong." Then he said "Jesus, remember me when you come into your kingdom." Jesus answered him, "Truly I tell you, today you will be with me in paradise." (Luke 23:27-43 NIV)

When they kept on questioning him, he straightened up and said to them, "Let any one of you who is without sin be the first to throw a stone at her." (John 8:7 NIV)

Carry each other's burdens, and in this way you will fulfill the law of Christ. (Galatians 6:2 NIV)

For we know him who said, "It is mine to avenge; I will repay," and again, "The Lord will judge his people." (Heb. 10:30 NIV)

Cast all your anxiety on him because he cares for you. Be alert and of sober mind. Your enemy the devil prowls around like a roaring lion looking for someone to devour. Resist him, standing firm in the faith, because you know that the family of believers throughout the world is undergoing the same kind of sufferings. And the God of all grace, who called you to his eternal glory In Christ, after you have suffered a little while, will himself restore you and make you strong, firm and steadfast. To him be the power for ever and ever. Amen. *(1 Peter 5:7-11)*

And he who searches our hearts knows the mind of the Spirit, because the Spirit intercedes for God's people in accordance with the will of God. And we know that in all things God works for the good of those who love him, who have been called according to his purpose. For those God foreknew he also predestined to be conformed to the image of his Son, that he might be the firstborn among many brothers and sisters. And those he predestined, he also called; those he called, he also justified; those he justified, he also glorified. What, then, shall we say in response to these things? If God is for us, who can be against us? He who did not spare his own Son, but gave him up for us all-how will he not also, along with him, graciously give us all things? Who will bring any charge against those whom God has chosen? It is God who justifies. Who then is the one who condemns? No one. Christ Jesus who died-more than that, who was raised to life-is at the right hand of God and is also interceding for us. Who shall separate us from the love of Christ? Shall trouble or hardship or persecution or famine or nakedness or danger or sword? As it is written:" For your sake we face death all day long;

(Romans 8:27-39 NIV)

When I became a born-again believer, getting to know God became the most important thing in my life. Getting to know his ways, learning how he does things, how he felt and feels in certain situations. I had to know him personally. I didn't just want to know him only in one form, but as God the Father, God the Son and God the Holy Spirit. I wanted to know the truth, the whole truth, and nothing but the truth. It was important to know how he operated in this world and to learn of His righteousness.

At the beginning of my new birth, sometimes, while reading the bible and studying his word, I would become confused. It wasn't because I didn't understand what I was reading. I was getting a different understanding of what I had been taught or had heard prior to my new birth. This sometimes deeply disturbed me, being that I had attended church most of my childhood. I had attended Sunday school and teaching classes in the church. I had been under different leaders and taught by different teachers that I believed to be some of the best. There were also people (mentors) in the church that I looked up to and listened to. To me, their word was the truth, especially the Pastor's word.

I would begin to struggle within myself while studying the word of God. Wrestling with what I had always understood and what I was understanding now. I cried out, "Lord, take away all that I thought I knew, and you teach me afresh your word and your way, your righteousness" *(Matt 6:33)*. I wanted to know the truth.

I also begin to pray for him to give me wisdom from heaven. Somehow I knew I wouldn't be able to learn the truth without it

(James 1:5). I desired to know him in every way that he would allow me to. I began to search the scriptures diligently. Flipping the pages with expectancy as I studied, knowing that I would find the answer to every question that I asked.

The more I studied, the more questions I seemed to have like: How did he feel when his disciples left him, and Peter denied him? I got that answer, but that's another story. And how could he love us when we were the reason his son suffered and died *(Isaiah 53:3-12)*. How can he counsel us and be so concerned for us still now? Me trying to process it with my human mind. I just couldn't really comprehend it. It was beyond my understanding how someone could love me so much. Then I would wonder how Jesus while suffering on the cross *(Luke 23:27-43)* still cared for and pleaded for and comforted the very ones that had a hand in His sufferings. It was beyond human comprehension, but I desired to know His heart and answer on these things. I don't know why it was so important for me to know. I don't know why it stayed on my heart and in my mind. I figured, as I said before, He was a teacher desiring to teach, and I was a student desiring to learn, so I chased after His heart.

I would not only study to learn of Him, but I would praise Him. I would sing love songs to Him. I loved to be in His presence. I would put on music and dance for Him. I didn't understand completely why then, but whatever I felt I was led to do, or should I say that I was compelled to do, I did. I wouldn't hold anything back when it came and being in His presence. I remember spending hours at a time in my house alone, just loving Him, praising Him, studying and meditating on His word, and talking to Him and listening for Him. Some Saturdays, I would tell Him I wanted to give Him back most of the day that He had given me. So, I would go out to the church, which was in the country. It was like my secret place. I knew no one would look for me there. I wanted to be alone with the Lord, just Him and me. No interruptions, no one taking up any of his time. I would go out to the church cleaning inside or working outside. Whichever I was doing, I would be inquiring of the Lord and listening for Him for answers to whatever I was inquiring about. Before I knew it, the day would be almost gone. Although He answered most of the questions fairly quickly, there were those I still didn't understand enough. The question about loving us and counseling us was not yet satisfied within me.

We had grown to love each other. We were best friends. And every now and then, I would ponder how He could love me so much in my unworthy state. Me being the reason he suffered and died; I just couldn't understand. Still looking at the mystery of salvation through human eyes and thinking about it with a carnal mind. And I didn't know why it kept coming up before me. Maybe He would place it there. Maybe He desired for me to know how much He loved me or wanted me to understand the depth of that love. Maybe He wanted me to not just know that He loved me, but His heart on the matter, the truth of the matter.

Time passed, and my relationship grew stronger and closer with the Lord. He had become my everything. There was nothing I wouldn't do or give up for Him. I didn't want anything to come between us, nothing! He had become my everything. Whatever I needed, He was it and still is. Even though I still wasn't sure how and why He loved me so. I had learned His love was unconditional. I had even learned the name for that kind of love. "Agape." But yet and still I wasn't clear on how He did it. I just kept on accepting it. The love he gives. He loves me like no other. And there is nothing that can compare to being in His presence.

So, I began to lose a lot to keep my relationship with Him. I lost friends, family, material possessions, even my husband at the time. Basically, I lost most of the things that were important to me. He became most important in my life, other than my daughter. I had to live to please Him, to hear from Him and know Him.

So, a few years passed, and although our relationships became stronger, so did the trials and troubles. Suffering through a few, I began to trust Him more and more. I knew He could bring me through anything. And as I saw my loved ones suffer every now and then, I remember telling Him I would rather go through than them. And I just didn't like seeing them suffer. I would rather suffer than see them suffer. Not that I had so much confidence in myself. But I had that much confidence in the Lord.

I had suffered many things. The enemy being so angry because of our (The Lord and I) relationship. But I didn't care, as long as the Lord was still there. My life with Christ was good, and all seemed to be well. Then tragedy struck. I suffered the passing of my only child. There was an accident that occurred, and it had cost me, my daughter. There were others involved: a young man and young woman.

Since I had come to know the Lord, and He had taught me so much about life. He had taught me His ways and word in a way that man could not have taught me. Right away, I recognized who was really to blame for the loss of my daughter. I realized that it was the enemy *(1 Peter 5:8)*. So I realized who was behind this tribulation. Although I knew who was to blame, others in the family were not as knowledgeable. And because of it, the enemy tried to wreak havoc through our family.

The situation was so complexed. There were a lot of hurt feelings in my family. And with me knowing and understanding this, my compassion (love) for them became more important than my grief.

You see, about two weeks prior to my daughter's passing away. She came to me one evening and told me she was ready for a change. And all I knew to tell her was about Jesus. That He was the only one who could make a significant change in her life, and she was more than willing. The Lord also confirmed the change through conversations we had (me and my daughter) the last two weeks of her life here. So I knew she was in a better and safe place. I knew she yet still lived *(John 3:16)*.

Knowing all that the Lord had shown me, I was determined not to allow the enemy (devil) the victory. He would not come to destroy all that our family had accomplished to become one family. So I was ready for war. Still following after the Lord, when the tragedy happened. It seemed as if he just stood there, and as I kept walking (spiritually speaking), I stepped right inside of him. And he became my hiding place and began to operate through me. I found myself doing things that I could never have done on my own. As a matter of fact, it wasn't me at all. It was him. And I knew it was him.

I can give you some examples. The young man that played a part in my daughter's passing sent word for me to come. He was in jail, and he wanted me to come to the jail. So I did. He began to sob uncontrollably, telling me he was sorry, and he needed to know he was forgiven by me. And with me knowing that he was sorry. And that he was a victim to the works of the enemy; He was already forgiven as far as I was concerned. And he also prayed the prayer of repentance with me.

I witness through conversations with others (family, friends, etc.) that there was a lot of hate towards him. I'd seen the enemy trying to manifest in all sorts of people and ways. He was trying to take this tragedy to create even more tragedies. With me knowing this, I began to ask the Lord what we should do. So I was instructed to write an article and place it in the paper for all to read who would read. Just to let people know that it was more to the situation than most could see or understand. And that we were not to judge, and that we must forgive. I wanted to remind those that were already believers that we are to remain being believers (representing Christ) in the hard times as we did in the good times. And those that had not yet become believers (not representing Christ), to take a good look at their lives in hope for them to want to live for Him also *(John 8:7)*. Another example was a young lady, whom I love. I witness her sorrow and grief that she inherited from the tragedy. She too, was a victim of the devil's cunning schemes in the passing of my daughter. I hold no unforgiveness towards her. For she too was already forgiven, with me knowing who the enemy was.

Although others would try and encourage and comfort her. And some showed some sign that they didn't hold it against her. I

131

knew it was most important that she knew that I had forgiven her. Every now and then, she would come to me, pouring all her emotions upon me, expressing her remorse. And I would try my best to comfort her, just the way I would want to be treated if I were in the position she was in at the time.

Then there were those (other family members) from both sides that would call saying they were thinking of me, and I would end up comforting them *(Galatians 6:2)*. Whatever anyone needed that I could provide at the time, I would give if I had it to give. Whether it was comfort, counsel, or my services. I gave whatever I had to give.

There were even those who wanted to get vengeance against the young man. Which I understood it was because of the deep hurt and anger, which is a part of grieving. But I prayed to God to hold it back because it did not belong to them. It belonged to Him (God) *(Heb. 10:30)*.

After some time passed, while still in the process of fighting against all the turmoil that the enemy tried to cause, I began to become burdened down. I began to grieve. I needed to get away from it all. And I knew what I needed to do. I needed to be in my secret place alone with the Lord. I needed to cry to Him and allow Him to comfort me *(1 Peter 5:7-11)* because he was the only one that could. So I began to ask Him. Why couldn't I focus on my daughter's passing? I knew I loved her more than anyone else other than Him. And why did it seem I had to be more concerned about everyone else than myself. Why is it that I must comfort and counsel others in their grief when I'm the one that should be grieving the most? I'm the one that needs comfort and counseling the most.

As the questions rolled on, I heard a still soft voice answer, "That's what I did," and "that's what I do." It was said in such a humble way. As if he was asking me at the same time, would I stay or would I walk away? Because of how He had answered me. You see, He had answered my questions about love and how he loves; through this tragedy and all the people it had affected. He taught me a lesson about His ways through the manifestation of His agape love through me. He allowed me to see through the passing of my daughter that He was making me to become more like Him. So, I saw through His eyes and considered the situations through His mind, and I experienced compassion (love) through His heart. He gave me His agape love for those who were responsible for my daughter's death. He took all that the devil meant for bad and used it for the good. As I surrendered unto His will; He manifested Himself, that others would see Him at work in my life. And my question about His Love was satisfied, He deserves all the honor, all the praise and all the glory, for what He does to, for, and through me *(Romans8:27-39)*.

A Word of Wisdom

As you read this story, I hope you read it attentively.

Letting go of the carnal, giving way to the spiritual, that you

may see all that you can see. You read of heartbreak, struggles,

confusion and trouble, the true enemy and grief.

But in all of your getting, get understanding, that you may live a

life of higher quality. For a moment, forgetting all evil, not

judging people. And focus on what you're probably ignoring

And see what the story is showing.

It's not about all the things mentioned above.

But it's about God's Agape Love.

So, don't focus on the tragedy in this story.

But focus on the manifestation of God and His glory,

Because whether through experience or reading the story

We all play a part.

So, reflect back to when you were reading,

What you were feeling in your heart.

Looking at all the characters, actions, attitudes and speech,

While searching yourself in all honesty

Realizing what your part would be.

Were you a part of what the devil tried to achieve?

Or a part of God's unconditional love, Agape?

Trails and tribulation come in many ways.

We never know what the day may bring.

Remember this story of God's glory taught by the Lord to me.

And if you didn't before now you know,

That His Agape love He must show.

So do your part and let Him into your heart.

For this is the right thing to do.

When weary, submit to His will, sit in His presence and be still.

That He may manifest Himself through you

Then you will better understand and appreciate the story,

Of Agape love and God in His Glory.

Hear My Voice

"The gatekeeper opens the gate for him and the sheep listen to his voice. He calls his own sheep by name and leads them out. When he has brought out his own, he goes on ahead of them, and his sheep follow him because they know his voice. (John 10:3-4 NIV)

"Jesus answered: 'Watch out that no one deceives you. (Matthew 24:4 NIV)

"You are a king, then!" said Pilate. Jesus answered, "You say that I am a king. In fact, the reason I was born and came into the world is to testify to the truth. Everyone on the side of truth listens to me." (John 18:37 NIV)

"Here I am! I stand at the door and knock. If anyone hears my voice and opens the door, I will come in and eat with that person, and they with me." (Revelation 3:20 NIV)

"Dear friend, I pray that you may enjoy good health and that all my go well with you, even as your soul is getting along well." (3 John 2 NIV)

"Very truly I tell you, whoever hears my word and believes him who sent me has eternal life and will not be judged but has crossed over from death to life. Very truly I tell you, a time is coming and has now come when the dead will hear the voice of the Son of God and those who hear will live."
(John 5:24-25 NIV)

I had a daughter. Her name was Tiffany. She became the most important person in my life when I gave birth to her. As I looked upon that beautiful, sweet face while I held her in my arms. I realized I was responsible for a baby, an adolescent, a teen in a sense, an adult, but most of all, a soul. Wow! What a responsibility. I made a promise to her that day that I would do my best to impart all the good I could in her while I had the chance. I would teach her to be the best person she could be, no matter what age she was in whatever part of her life she was in. I would teach her the best qualities in life and the most important things in and about life.

I remember a time when we were discussing a matter, and there were other family members and friends around. As I tried my best to give her the best advice I could, some of the others would interrupt me, giving their opinion going against my advice. I noticed how she would stop hearing me and listen to those that would speak out. Realizing at that time, if I was going to be able to keep my promise to her that I made (when I first held her in my arms), she would have to know hearing me was more important than hearing what everyone else would have to say. So, a few days later, she came to me with the matter again, and I asked her, "what did I tell you the other day?" and I gave her the advice again. She responded, "Oh, I didn't hear you because there were too many people talking." I said, "If there are a thousand people in a room talking, and I'm one of them, this is the voice you better hear!" I taught my daughter to learn to listen to my voice that day. After that day, it didn't matter where we were or who we were around. No matter what age she was, when I spoke, she would shut out everyone else, giving me her full attention, and she would hear my voice.

That day I also learned how important it was for me to hear the voice of God *(John 10:3-4)*. With so many voices speaking out. So many teachers and preachers. So many denominations, religious beliefs. So many different theologies of men. So many voices speaking in the world today *(Matt 24:4)*. Then I heard the Lord say, "If there are a thousand voices speaking, and I am one of them, this is one voice you better hear." From that day forward, I began listening for the voice of God no matter where I was, who I was around, or what was going on *(John 18:37)*. No matter where He speaks, or how He speaks. I have learned to listen for His voice *(Rev. 3:20)*. For He is wisdom, He wishes to impart in us all the good He can before it's too late. He wants to be responsible for our souls if we let Him. He wants us to be the best we can be, no matter what age we are *(3 John 2)*. He wants to teach us, but in order for Him to do that, His voice is one voice we must hear *(John 5:24-25)*.

A Word of Wisdom

In this world there is so much chatter,

Voices speaking out on every matter.

As we listen, let us learn to let no other voice interfere,

that when God speaks amongst all the chatter

His voice is the voice we will be sure to hear.

Listen for Wisdom's Cry

"Out in the open wisdom calls aloud, she raises her voice in the public square; on top of the wall she cries out, at the city gate she makes her speech." (Proverbs 1:20-21 NIV)

"If any of you lacks wisdom, you should ask God, who gives generously to all without finding fault, and it will be given to you." (James 1:5 NIV)

*"Blessed are those who find wisdom, those who gain understanding, for she is more profitable than silver and yields better returns than gold. She is more precious than rubies; nothing you desire can compare with her. Long life is in her right hand; in her left hand are riches and honor. Her ways are pleasant ways, and all her paths are peace. She is a tree of life to those who take hold of her; those who hold her fast will be blessed. By wisdom the Lord laid the earth's foundations, by understanding he set the heavens in place; by his knowledge the watery depths were divided, and the clouds let drop the dew."
(Proverbs 3:13-20 NIV)*

"Does not wisdom call out? Does not understanding raise her voice? At the highest point along the way, where the gate leading into the city, at the entrance, she cries aloud: 'To you, O people, I call out: I raise my voice to all mankind. You who are simple, gain prudence; you who are foolish, set your hearts on it. Listen,

for I have trustworthy things to say: I open my lips to speak what is right. My mouth speaks what is true, for my lips detest wickedness. All the words of my mouth are just; none of them is crooked or perverse. To the discerning all of them are right; they are upright to those who have found knowledge. Choose my instruction instead of silver, knowledge rather than choice gold, for wisdom is more precious than rubies, and nothing you desire can compare with her. 'I wisdom, dwell together with prudence; I possess knowledge and discretion. To fear the Lord is to hate evil; I hate pride and arrogance, evil behavior and perverse speech. Counsel and sound judgment are mine; I have insight, I have power. By me kings reign and rulers issue decrees that are just; by me princes govern, and nobles-all who rule on earth. I love those who love me, and those who seek me find me. With me are riches and honor, enduring wealth and prosperity. My fruit is better than fine gold; what I yield surpasses choice silver. I walk in the way of righteousness, along the paths of justice, bestowing a rich inheritance on those who love me and making their treasuries full. The Lord brought me forth as the first of his works, before his deed of old; I was formed long ages ago, at the very beginning, when the world came to be. When there were no watery depths, I was given birth, before he made the world or its fields or any of the dust of the earth. I was there when he set the heavens in place, when he marked out the horizon on the face of the deep, when he established the clouds above and fixed securely the fountains of the deep, when he gave the sea its boundary so the waters would not overstep his command, and when he marked out the foundations of the earth. Then I was constantly at his side. I was filled with delight day after day, rejoicing in his whole world and delighting in mankind. Now then, my children, listen to me; blessed are those who keep my ways. Listen to my instruction and be wise; do not disregard it. Blessed are those who listen to me, watching daily at my doors, waiting at my doorway. For those who find me find life and receive favor from the Lord. But those who fail to find me harm themselves; all who hate me love death.' (Proverbs 8 NIV)

There was a time in my life when I began to focus on rocks. As I have said before, I really didn't know why at the time. But as I focused on them, the shape of some of them were a likeness to some animals or different parts of animals. For instance, some rocks would be in the shape of a seal or the shape of the head of an animal, etc. So, seeing this, I began to make rock animals. I made a seal, whale, hen and chicks, penguin, turtles, and all sorts of animals. I would gather the rocks, bond them together, and paint them, watching them appear to come alive. But I didn't stop there.

I began to attach signs to them. On the penguin, I would put a sign telling how Jesus loves all the children of the world, red, yellow, black, and white. Of course, the penguin was black and white. I also made turtles, attaching a sign with the scripture about the race is not given to the swift but to those that endureth to the end. I also took a big rock with other small rocks and created a scene of flowers, ladybugs, and a rabbit hiding in an indention of the big rock. Then I wrote on the big rock, "Rock of ages cleft for me let me hide myself on thee. This was my favorite. There were many more rock figures that I made with attached messages.

I began to give them out to people and sitting some around in my home and yard for people to see when passing by. Although I enjoyed doing different kinds of crafts, this was one of my favorites. Because as I gathered the rocks, bonding them together, painting them, watching them unfold (appearing to come alive). Another revelation began to unfold as I attached the signs with the scriptures and different phrases to the rock figures. It was an example of the rocks crying out. Not only in word, but also a picture or example of the word. It was a message within itself.

I began to see how wisdom does cry out *(Proverbs 1:20-21)*. Wisdom cries out in many ways through many things in many places. Wisdom cries out for many reasons as instruction, as guidance, as comfort, an answer to a question, or prayer and much more. The Bible tells us to ask for wisdom *(James 1:5)* to desire wisdom, to search for wisdom, to get wisdom, to keep wisdom, and forget her not.

It tells us that wisdom is the principal thing. The merchandise of it is better than the merchandise of silver, and the gain thereof than fine gold. Her (wisdom) ways are pleasantness, and all her paths are peace. She is life to those that get her and happiness to the one that retains her *(Proverbs 3:13-20)*. Wisdom is all this and more. Wisdom cries out to us in all sorts of ways, and without it, we are not able to get understanding. Wisdom cries out to us, desiring to teach us about life. She (wisdom) cries out in a way that is comprehensible to anyone who will listen. Wisdom is essential to our understanding of who God is. There is no other word that can come closer to defining who God is than "Wisdom." Therefore, we could never comprehend totally who He is in this life because "wisdom" in it is completeness extends beyond this life. Wisdom was (before the foundation of this world) wisdom is and always will be *(Proverbs 8)*. It has no beginning, and it has no end. It is the highest degree of knowing. And only God in his awesomeness holds it. Wanting to impart a portion of it into the hearts and minds of his people. He cries out through wisdom. But do we listen? Do we listen for wisdom's cry? Do we listen in a way that we can hear? Do we limit Him in His crying out to us? Do we search for wisdom diligently?

With all our going, desires, learning, business. With all our hearing, living, working, meeting, growing, teaching, preaching, giving, etc. In all that we do in this life, let us not forget the principal things. Let us not forget to ask for wisdom from God. And when we ask, let us with anticipation listen, receiving it in whatever way He desires to give it—not limiting him with a carnal mind, allowing Him to teach us His truth, His righteousness, and His ways. In whatever way, it may be. Learning to listen for wisdom's cry. That comes from a teacher of the highest degree.

About the Author

Tommy (Tommie) J. Jackson was born in a small town (Muleshoe, Texas) and later raised in Clovis, New Mexico by her parents.

Tommie accepted Christ as her Lord and Saviour at a very young age, around seven years old, in a theater. After watching a movie at a free show featured for children, an invitation to discipleship was given; with a convicted heart, Tommie accepted.

As a wearer of many hats, she has been a business owner, Finance secretary for a District

Women's Auxiliary, Teacher and counselor for recovering women at a local mission, teacher for a Young Women's Auxiliary, Sunday School teacher, Training union teacher, Choir director at her previous. She now serves as Prayer Coordinator, Evangelism Director, serves on the welcoming committee amongst other services in her local Church and community.

She is a wife, a mother, a grandmother and a friend. But most important, she is a Child of God who is deeply passionate about sharing the word of God in a way that the highly educated to the most uneducated can understand. Her sole purpose in this life is to live a life for Christ that it may point people to Him.

Connect with Tommie on Social Media

Facebook: Tommie Jackson